C000303188

THOMAS HARDY

Tom Paulin was born in Leeds in 1949 but grew up in Belfast, and was educated at the universities of Hull and Oxford. He has published nine collections of poetry, of which the most recent is *Love's Bonfire* (2012), as well as several critical works including *The Day-Star of Liberty: William Hazlitt's Radical Style* (1998) and *Crusoe's Secret: The Aesthetics of Dissent* (2005).

In the Faber Nature Poets collection

JOHN CLARE – Poems selected by Paul Farley
SAMUEL TAYLOR COLERIDGE – Poems selected by James Fenton
JOHN KEATS – Poems selected by Andrew Motion
THOMAS HARDY – Poems selected by Tom Paulin
EDWARD THOMAS – Poems selected by Matthew Hollis
WILLIAM WORDSWORTH – Poems selected by Seamus Heaney

THOMAS HARDY
Poems selected by TOM PAULIN

FABER & FABER

First published in 2001
by Faber & Faber Ltd
Bloomsbury House
74–77 Great Russell Street
London WC1B 3DA

This edition published in 2016

Printed in Great Britain by
CPI Group (UK) Ltd, Croydon, CR0 4YY

A CIP record for this book
is available from the British Library

ISBN 978–0–571–32875–8

FSC
www.fsc.org
MIX
Paper from
responsible sources
FSC® C101712

10 9 8 7 6 5 4 3 2 1

Contents

Introduction

In his mid-eighties, Thomas Hardy observed another spring and set it down in fluently graceful verse:

> The thrushes sing as the sun is going,
>   And the finches whistle in ones and pairs,
> And as it gets dark loud nightingales
>   In bushes
> Pipe, as they can when April wears,
>   As if all Time were theirs.

Characteristically, he sets that relaxed, gently admiring line 'As if all Time were theirs', against the mercantile adjective 'brand-new' in the second stanza:

> These are brand-new birds of twelve-months' growing,
> Which a year ago, or less than twain,
> No finches were, nor nightingales,
>   Nor thrushes,
> But only particles of grain,
>   And earth, and air, and rain.

Here he is remembering a passage from a novel he wrote more than thirty years earlier, for in *Tess* we read that:

> The season developed and matured. Another year's instalment of flowers, leaves, nightingales, thrushes, finches and such ephemeral creatures, took up their positions where only a year ago others had stood in their place, when these were nothing more than germs and inorganic particles. Rays from the sunrise drew forth the buds and stretched them into long stalks, lifted up sap in noiseless streams, opened petals, and sucked out scents in invisible jets and breathings.

'Instalment' and 'brand-new' belong to the language of consumer capitalism. Nature is a biological conveyor belt which is always predictable, always on time. As a young man, Hardy read *The Origin of Species* along with Hume's argument against miracles, which explains that there is always a 'natural solution' to any apparent miracle. He is remembering this reading here.

As an old man, he read books about Einstein and the new physics, and I've come to believe that the last-minute coup which the final couplet of this poem pulls off owes something to that reading:

> But only particles of grain,
> > And earth, and air, and rain.

Is he thinking of atomic particles? It would be anachronistic to suggest that he is imagining some kind of benign nuclear explosion, but like a conjurer he is extracting something miraculous from what seems to be a piece of perfectly competent light verse. He is suddenly making it into a true poem, and it is worth examining how his ever-so-delicate ear enables him to give us a moment of such pure *poesis*. Because the penultimate line sandwiches a bisyllable and a trisyllable between monosyllables it moves quickly, and this contrasts with the slower monosyllables in the last line, their unfolding slowness further arrested by the pausal commas. More than that the *k* in 'particles' touches the *g* in 'grain' (the two sounds are cognate), so that in retrospect one imagines this tactile nudge as that of a sperm locking onto an ovum.

This isn't merely fanciful, because the nouns in the last line are all contained in 'grain' from which they effectively burst out. Thus the *guh* in 'grain' begets the *uh* in 'earth', while the remaining letters of 'grain' spin out into 'air' and 'rain'. To return to fashionable commodity-speak, Hardy 'unpacks' the word in order to unfold his last, surprising, lovely line in front of us. Out of his reading of Schopenhauer, he is giving us an example of the knowledge and freedom, the *Vorstellung*, which can transcend the routine, mechanical workings of the Will, which is sex, biological process, predictable change of season.

We can see a similar moment of impulsive, joyous freedom in Louis MacNeice's 'Order to View':

It was a big house, bleak;
Grass on the drive;
We had been there before
But memory, weak in front of
A blistered door, could find
Nothing alive now;
The shrubbery dripped, a crypt
Of leafmould dreams; a tarnished
Arrow over an empty stable
Shifted a little in the tenuous wind,

And wishes were unable
To rise; on the garden wall
The pear trees had come loose
From rotten loops; one wish,
A rainbow bubble, rose,
Faltered, broke in the dull
Air – What was the use?
The bell-pull would not pull
And the whole place, one might
Have supposed, was deadly ill:
The world was closed,

And remained closed until
A sudden angry tree
Shook itself like a setter
Flouncing out of a pond
And beyond the sombre line
Of limes a cavalcade
Of clouds rose like a shout of
Defiance. Near at hand
Somewhere in a loose-box

A horse neighed
And all the curtains flew out of
The windows; the world was open.

March, 1940.

Where MacNeice shows dullness transformed into an
anarchic kick against routine which is also like a promise of
early victory in Europe, Hardy more often stays remorselessly
with dullness, and paints its grey on grey. In his most
accomplished early poem, 'Neutral Tones', which he wrote
nearly sixty years before 'Proud Songsters', he builds the
dreary scene through ashen images and a series of anapaests
which rather than speeding the lines, seem to slow them
down:

We stood by a pond that winter day,
And the sun was white, as though chidden of God,
And a few leaves lay on the starving sod;
   – They had fallen from an ash, and were gray.

The next two stanzas are more conventional: 'Your eyes on
me were as eyes that rove/ Over tedious riddles of years ago.'
But the reprise of the opening stanza in the last two lines
makes this one of the definitive Victorian lyrics:

Since then, keen lessons that love deceives,
And wrings with wrong, have shaped to me
Your face, and the God-curst sun, and a tree,
   And a pond edged with grayish leaves.

The first two lines are samey, predictable – we have to expect
this in Hardy, he can throw the clunky, the naffly sentimental,
in with the most inspired and unexpected lines. It's as though
the predictable Victorianese and the expertly cadenced
spontaneity depend on each other, are somehow in consort,
married. And we know that Hardy is the poet and the
chronicler of marriage's and love's deceptions.

In the final stanza, it's almost as though he has to set up a pompously confident actorly voice, which with that facile alliteration 'wrings with wrong' and obvious syntax has the glib sonority of a young man trying to sound old and disillusioned. Then he makes a new rhythm – the rhythm of the natural, concentrated speaking voice, against the plummy preceding lines. The pausal commas are like bullets, or perhaps more accurately the three phrases in the third line are like three deliberate, unhurried shots. And though the last line appears to be a single, unbroken sweep of desolation, it breaks the rules of metre to subtly repeat the trinal structure of the previous line:

And a pónd / edǵed / with gŕayish leáves

After the anapaest, which picks up the earlier anapaest, the verb 'edged' is out on its own – it doesn't belong to any metrical foot. There follow two iambs which make a single unit of sense and sound. Hardy had a deep knowledge of metrics, and part of the fun of his poems lies in watching him use sometimes rare and complex verse forms – he likes the exercise and challenge of form, though this is his way of pointing to the experiments with rhythm that he is making elsewhere.

He is also a wonderfully allusive poet, and in 'Neutral Tones' he is rewriting the soppiness of Arnold's closing lines to 'Dover Beach':

Ah, love, let us be true
To one another! for the world, which seems
To lie before us like a land of dreams,
So various, so beautiful, so new,
Hath really neither joy, nor love, nor light,
Nor certitude, nor peace, nor help for pain;
And we are here as on a darkling plain
Swept with confused alarms of struggle and flight,
Where ignorant armies clash by night.

Hardy's wintry pond is Arnold's darkling plain, it is an

intellectual as well as an emotional image of scepticism, loss of faith, that sense of eviction from the consolations of traditional religion. Behind it stands Job, and before it the tortured scholar, Jude.

The tricks and shifts in rhythm in Hardy's finest poems mean that we are kept constantly alert to the innumerable voices that lie behind and within his lines. In 'Voices from Things Growing in a Churchyard', the timidity of Fanny Hurd's voice, the gruff, no-nonsense manliness of Bachelor Bowring consort with the sexiness of the much-kissed Eve Greensleeves' voice. While in another poem, 'Transformations', on the same humanist, wittily materialist subject, Hardy begins with formal incantatory trochees:

> Portion of this yew
> Is a man my grandsire knew,
> Bosomed here at its foot:

As if sensing that this rhythm runs the danger of being too grandly pompous, he switches into nimbler iambics:

> This branch may be his wife,
> A ruddy human life
> Now turned to a green shoot.

It's as if the wife has escaped from a dark, imprisoning marriage and is having a love affair – the clutching spondees and that green shoot in the last line are randily locked together, while that adjective 'ruddy' is picked up and transformed by 'turned' and 'green'. Like Stanley Spencer's *Resurrection*, this is a visionary English graveyard.

In the second stanza, Hardy plays on the sense of 'know' as carnal knowledge and turns the masculinist sense of 'enter' back on itself to emphasize the unnamed girl's triumphant, reasserted virginity:

> These grasses must be made
> Of her who often prayed,

Last century, for repose;
And the fair girl long ago
Whom I often tried to know
May be entering this rose.

Notice how the last four rhymes chime on 'o' – the abounding 'nerves and veins' in the last stanza are anticipated by the vaginal sign and the hint of the demure perfect cheeks of an English rose.

As so often in Hardy, this is a meditation on time and memory, subjects which are central to the lengthy poem 'The Abbey Mason', where the witty octosyllabic couplets speak gnomically of the hidden sources of his art. In the central section of the poem, the architect faces a problem he cannot solve:

'This long-vogued style is quite outworn!

The upper archmould nohow serves
To meet the lower tracery curves:

The ogees bend too far away
To give the flexures interplay.'

Hardy the one-time architect lovingly places the technical terms in his lines, and puns on lines of verse and lines on an architectural drawing. In a note included in *The Life and Work of Thomas Hardy*, his third-person autobiography ostensibly written by his second wife Florence, he makes this tantalizing connection between poetry and architecture:

Years earlier he had decided that too regular a beat was bad art. He had fortified himself in his opinion by thinking of the analogy of architecture, between which art and that of poetry he had discovered, to use his own words, that there existed a close and curious parallel, both arts, unlike some others, having to carry a rational content inside their artistic form. He knew that in architecture cunning irregularity is of enormous worth, and it is obvious that he carried on into his verse, perhaps in part unconsciously, the Gothic art-principle in which he had been trained – the principle of spontaneity, found in mouldings, tracery, and such like – resulting in the 'unforeseen' (as it has been called) character of his metres and stanzas, that of stress rather than of syllable, poetic texture rather than poetic veneer; the latter kind of thing, under the name of 'constructed ornament', being what he, in common with every Gothic student, had been taught to avoid as the plague. He shaped his poetry accordingly, introducing metrical pauses, and reversed beats; and found for his trouble that some particular line of a poem exemplifying this principle was greeted with a would-be jocular remark that such a line 'did not make for immortality'. The same critic might have gone to one of our cathedrals (to follow up the analogy of architecture), and on discovering that the carved leafage of some capital or spandrel in the best period of Gothic art strayed freakishly out of its bounds over the moulding, where by rule it had no business to be, or that the enrichments of a string-course were not accurately spaced; or that there was a sudden blank in a wall where a window was to be expected from formal measurement, have declared with equally merry conviction, 'This does not make for immortality.'

In 'The Abbey Mason' the architect or master mason has a sudden epiphany:

Scattering the rushes of the floor
He wandered from the chamber door

And sought the sizing pile, whereon
Struck dimly a cadaverous dawn

Through freezing rain, that drenched the board
Of diagram-lines he last had scored –

Chalked phantasies in vain begot
To knife the architectural knot –

In front of which he dully stood,
Regarding them in hopeless mood.

He closelier looked; then looked again:
The chalk-scratched draught-board faced the rain,

Whose icicled drops deformed the lines
Innumerous of his lame designs,

So that they streamed in small white threads
From the upper segments to the heads

Of arcs below, uniting them
Each by a stalactitic stem.

– At once, with eyes that struck out sparks,
He adds accessory cusping-marks,

Then laughs aloud. The thing was done
So long assayed from sun to sun. . . .

A rain-stained architectural drawing, like the rain-stained sketchpads in other poems, is his symbol for the action of time, chance and memory on the imagination. Playing against the easy fluency of the octosyllabic couplet, Hardy throws in six abrasive stresses in 'The chálk-scrátched draúght-boárd fáced the raín'. A line which pays tribute to Browning's 'the quick sharp scratch/ And blue flare of a lighted match' in 'Meeting at Night', one of the most erotic Victorian poems. What we find in both poets is a fascination with fricative, abrasive, scratchy, dissonant sounds. It's as if they want to take a wire brush to any settled mellifluous sonic surface – they want to be true to the Gothic art principle of surprise and spontaneity. If English Gothic is one of the great embodiments of English liberty – and it is – so the work of both Browning and Hardy endlessly embodies the soaring, sometimes cranky creativity of that freedom-loving imagination.

In Hardy, there is a fondness for technical, odd, out-of-the way vocabulary, as in the next couplet where, in an implicit twist to Hume's phrase, the mason is inspired by the natural solution to the problem:

– At once, with eyes that struck out sparks,
He adds accessory cusping-marks.

It is a distinctive part of Hardy's 'craft-wit' to be able to draw on such ungainly phrases as 'accessory cusping-marks' and make them graceful. He does the same thing in this passage from *Tess of the D'Urbervilles*:

When Izz Huett and Tess arrived at the scene of operations only a rustling denoted that others had preceded them; to which, as the light increased, there were presently added the silhouettes of two men on the summit. They were busily 'unhaling' the rick, that is, stripping off the thatch before beginning to throw down the sheaves; and while this was in progress Izz and Tess, with the other women-workers in their whitey-brown pinners, stood waiting and shivering, Farmer Groby having insisted upon their being upon the spot thus early, to get the job over if possible by the end of the day. Close under the eaves of the stack, and as yet barely visible was the red tyrant that the women had come to serve – a timber-framed construction, with straps and wheels appertaining – the threshing-machine, which, whilst it was going, kept up a despotic demand upon the endurance of their muscles and nerves.

That plodding word 'appertaining' feels just right in this passage, which is constructed like a naïf painting, and is a piece of deftly perfect prose.

Tess's voice is caught in 'Tess's Lament', which needs to be heard in the Wessex voice that Barbara Jefford adopts in her definitive reading of the poem:

I would that folk forgot me quite,
　　　　Forgot me quite!
I would that I could shrink from sight,
　　　　And no more see the sun.
Would it were time to say farewell,
To claim my nook, to need my knell,
Time for them all to stand and tell
　　　　O' my day's work as done.

Ah! dairy where I lived so long,
　　　　I lived so long;
Where I would rise up stanch and strong,
　　　　And lie down hopefully.
'Twas there within the chimney-seat
He watched me to the clock's slow beat –
Loved me, and learnt to call me Sweet,
　　　　And whispered words to me.

There is a perfectly placed molossus – three strong stresses –
in 'clóck's slów beát' – while the strangeness of 'And
whispered words to me' reminds us that Angel Clare would
have addressed fanciful, strange, polysyllabic words in a
refined accent to her. He would have acted like the seducer
Alec d'Urberville, and violated the ingenuous, trusting young
woman whose innocence and vulnerability are so hauntingly
caught in this line.

Hardy's tender sensitivity to the human voice is at the core
of his imagination, and with that goes an attentiveness to the
pause, as in the moment after 'Sweet' that we need to prolong
ever so slightly more than the line-endings in the rest of the
stanza. Nowhere is this more audible and remarkable than in
this stanza from 'To Lizbie Browne':

Dear Lizbie Browne,
Where are you now?
In sun, in rain? –
Past joy, past pain,
Dear Lizbie Browne?

Sweet Lizbie Browne,
How you could smile,
How you could sing! –
How archly wile
In glance-giving,
Sweet Lizbie Browne!

And, Lizbie Browne,
Who else had hair
Bay-red as yours,
Or flesh so fair
Bred out of doors,
Sweet Lizbie Browne?

When, Lizbie Browne,
You had just begun
To be endeared
By stealth to one,
You disappeared,
My Lizbie Browne!

Ay, Lizbie Browne,
So swift your life,
And mine so slow,
You were a wife
Ere I could show
Love, Lizbie Browne.

That pause after 'show' – that marvellously slowed enjamb-
ment and the massive, grave stress it places on 'Love' – is quite
simply momentous (there is a great reading of the poem by
Dylan Thomas). One of Hardy's masterpieces, the poem
wittily repeats the name Lizbie Browne as a type of double or
sandwiching refrain, so that it becomes obsessive, tender,
impossible, lispy or labial, but wholly unkissable.

If we consider, how Hardy writes, to use George Herbert's
Anglican term 'pauseably', then these stanzas from 'At Castle

Boterel' detail the absolute, even transcendental quality of still moments of perfect silence:

> As I drive to the junction of lane and highway,
>   And the drizzle bedrenches the waggonette,
> I look behind at the fading byway,
>   And see on its slope, now glistening wet,
>   Distinctly yet
>
> Myself and a girlish form benighted
>   In dry March weather. We climb the road
> Beside a chaise. We had just alighted
>   To ease the sturdy pony's load
>   When he sighed and slowed.
>
> What we did as we climbed, and what we talked of
>   Matters not much, nor to what it led, –
> Something that life will not be balked of
>   Without rude reason till hope is dead,
>   And feeling fled.
>
> It filled but a minute. But was there ever
>   A time of such quality, since or before,
> In that hill's story? To one mind never,
>   Though it has been climbed, foot-swift, foot-sore,
>   By thousands more.

The three stresses on 'dry March weather', followed by the full stop, means that there is a definite long pause before the rest of the line gets under way. Another pause follows at the next full stop, another at the line ending. There is a particular emphatic pause after 'sighed', and we begin to understand that the 'quality' of the time they shared that 'filled but a minute' is being enacted by these pauses which punctuate the poem and which are so integral to the movement of the poem. This means that the poet's characteristic, concluding negative –

> And I shall traverse old love's domain
> > Never again

– is in its echoing of the earlier still moments rendered more complex, as if some immortal essence still survives.

The *Poems of 1912–13*, of which 'At Castle Boterel' is one of the most important poems, is an enduring memorial to Hardy's love for his first wife, Emma Lavinia Gifford, whom he met in Cornwall in 1870. In manuscript, this stanza from 'The Voice' was slightly different:

> Can it be you that I hear? Let me view you, then,
> Standing as when I drew near to the town
> Where you would wait for me: yes, as I knew you then,
> Even to the original air-blue gown!

Hardy had written in manuscript 'Even to the original hat and gown', but perhaps thinking this was nearly as banal as specifying that she carried a handbag, he changed the phrase. Now he could see the Virgin Mary in Emma's blue eyes. And he could see heaven, all eternity there, as well as the many Italian pictures he saw in the National Gallery which use the Marian colour, blue. He picks up the sound of the word in the penultimate line, 'Wind oozing thin through the thorn from norward', where the verb 'oozing' conflates the *z* in a 'breeze' in the previous stanza with the *oo* in 'blue', and the 'oo' in 'woman'. It's an eerie – and, yes, a convincingly ghostly – moment. Reading Hardy, we are always listening to the unique, the inscaped cadences of individual voices. And often the voices of the dead return to life in his lines.

Tom Paulin

THOMAS HARDY

Neutral Tones

We stood by a pond that winter day,
And the sun was white, as though chidden of God,
And a few leaves lay on the starving sod;
    – They had fallen from an ash, and were gray.

Your eyes on me were as eyes that rove
Over tedious riddles of years ago;
And some words played between us to and fro
    On which lost the more by our love.

The smile on your mouth was the deadest thing
Alive enough to have strength to die;
And a grin of bitterness swept thereby
    Like an ominous bird a-wing. . . .

Since then, keen lessons that love deceives,
And wrings with wrong, have shaped to me
Your face, and the God-curst sun, and a tree,
    And a pond edged with grayish leaves.

1867

Friends Beyond

William Dewy, Tranter Reuben, Farmer Ledlow late at
      plough,
    Robert's kin, and John's, and Ned's,
And the Squire, and Lady Susan, lie in Mellstock churchyard
      now!

'Gone,' I call them, gone for good, that group of local hearts
    and heads;
    Yet at mothy curfew-tide,
And at midnight when the noon-heat breathes it back from
      walls and leads,

They've a way of whispering to me – fellow-wight who yet
    abide –
    In the muted, measured note
Of a ripple under archways, or a lone cave's stillicide:

'We have triumphed: this achievement turns the bane to
    antidote,
    Unsuccesses to success,
Many thought-worn eves and morrows to a morrow free of
      thought.

'No more need we corn and clothing, feel of old terrestrial
    stress;
    Chill detraction stirs no sigh;
Fear of death has even bygone us: death gave all that we
      possess.'

W.D. – 'Ye mid burn the old bass-viol that I set such value
    by.'
Squire. – 'You may hold the manse in fee,
    You may wed my spouse, may let my children's
      memory of me die.'

Lady S. – 'You may have my rich brocades, my laces; take
　　each household key;
　　Ransack coffer, desk, bureau;
　Quiz the few poor treasures hid there, con the letters kept
　　by me.'

Far. – 'Ye mid zell my favourite heifer, ye mid let the
　　charlock grow,
　　Foul the grinterns, give up thrift.'
Far. Wife. – 'If ye break my best blue china, children, I shan't
　　care or ho.'

All. – 'We've no wish to hear the tidings, how the people's
　　fortunes shift;
　　What your daily doings are;
　Who are wedded, born, divided; if your lives beat slow or
　　swift.

'Curious not the least are we if our intents you make or mar,
　　If you quire to our old tune,
If the City stage still passes, if the weirs still roar afar.'

– Thus, with very gods' composure, freed those crosses late
　　and soon
　　Which, in life, the Trine allow
(Why, none witteth), and ignoring all that haps beneath the
　　moon,

William Dewy, Tranter Reuben, Farmer Ledlow late at
　　plough,
　　Robert's kin, and John's, and Ned's,
And the Squire, and Lady Susan, murmur mildly to me now.

The Impercipient

(*At a Cathedral Service*)

That with this bright believing band
　　I have no claim to be,
That faiths by which my comrades stand
　　Seem fantasies to me,
And　mirage-mists their Shining Land,
　　Is a strange destiny.

Why thus my soul should be consigned
　　To infelicity,
Why always I must feel as blind
　　To sights my brethren see,
Why joys they've found I cannot find,
　　Abides a mystery.

Since heart of mine knows not that ease
　　Which they know; since it be
That He who breathes All's Well to these
　　Breathes no All's-Well to me,
My lack might move their sympathies
　　And Christian charity!

I am like a gazer who should mark
　　An inland company
Standing unfingered, with, 'Hark! hark!
　　The glorious distant sea!'
And feel, 'Alas, 'tis but yon dark
　　And wind-swept pine to me!'

Yet I would bear my shortcomings
　　With meet tranquillity,
But for the charge that blessed things
　　I'd liefer not have be.
O, doth a bird deprived of wings
　　Go earth-bound wilfully!

6

Enough. As yet disquiet clings
About us. Rest shall we.

In a Eweleaze near Wetherbury

The years have gathered grayly
    Since I danced upon this leaze
With one who kindled gaily
    Love's fitful ecstasies!
But despite the term as teacher,
    I remain what I was then
In each essential feature
    Of the fantasies of men.

Yet I note the little chisel
    Of never-napping Time
Defacing wan and grizzel
    The blazon of my prime.
When at night he thinks me sleeping
    I feel him boring sly
Within my bones, and heaping
    Quaintest pains for by-and-by.

Still, I'd go the world with Beauty,
    I would laugh with her and sing,
I would shun divinest duty
    To resume her worshipping.
But she'd scorn my brave endeavour,
    She would not balm the breeze
By murmuring 'Thine for ever!'
    As she did upon this leaze.

1890

8

I Look Into My Glass

I look into my glass,
And view my wasting skin,
And say, 'Would God it came to pass
My heart had shrunk as thin!'

For then, I, undistrest
By hearts grown cold to me,
Could lonely wait my endless rest
With equanimity.

But Time, to make me grieve,
Part steals, lets part abide;
And shakes this fragile frame at eve
With throbbings of noontide.

Drummer Hodge

I

They throw in Drummer Hodge, to rest
    Uncoffined – just as found:
His landmark is a kopje-crest
    That breaks the veldt around;
And foreign constellations west
    Each night above his mound.

II

Young Hodge the Drummer never knew –
    Fresh from his Wessex home –
The meaning of the broad Karoo,
    The Bush, the dusty loam,
And why uprose to nightly view
    Strange stars amid the gloam.

III

Yet portion of that unknown plain
    Will Hodge for ever be;
His homely Northern breast and brain
    Grow to some Southern tree,
And strange-eyed constellations reign
    His stars eternally.

1899

To Lizbie Browne

I

Dear Lizbie Browne,
Where are you now?
In sun, in rain? –
Or is your brow
Past joy, past pain,
Dear Lizbie Browne?

II

Sweet Lizbie Browne,
How you could smile,
How you could sing! –
How archly wile
In glance-giving,
Sweet Lizbie Browne!

III

And, Lizbie Browne,
Who else had hair
Bay-red as yours,
Or flesh so fair
Bred out of doors,
Sweet Lizbie Browne?

IV

When, Lizbie Browne,
You had just begun
To be endeared
By stealth to one,
You disappeared,
My Lizbie Browne!

V

Ay, Lizbie Browne,
So swift your life,
And mine so slow,
You were a wife
Ere I could show
Love, Lizbie Browne.

VI

Still, Lizbie Browne,
You won, they said,
When you were wed. . . .
Where went you then,
O Lizbie Browne?

VII

Dear Lizbie Browne,
I should have thought,
'Girls ripen fast,'
And coaxed and caught
You ere you passed,
Dear Lizbie Browne!

VIII

But, Lizbie Browne,
I let you slip;
Shaped not a sign;
Touched never your lip
With lip of mine,
Lost Lizbie Browne!

IX

So, Lizbie Browne,
When on a day
Men speak of me
As not, you'll say,
'And who was he?' –
Yes, Lizbie Browne!

A Broken Appointment

> You did not come,
> And marching Time drew on, and wore me numb. –
> Yet less for loss of your dear presence there
> Than that I thus found lacking in your make
> That high compassion which can overbear
> Reluctance for pure lovingkindness' sake
> Grieved I, when, as the hope-hour stroked its sum,
> > You did not come.
>
> You love not me,
> And love alone can lend you loyalty;
> – I know and knew it. But, unto the store
> Of human deeds divine in all but name,
> Was it not worth a little hour or more
> To add yet this: Once you, a woman, came
> To soothe a time-torn man; even though it be
> > You love not me?

An August Midnight

I

A shaded lamp and a waving blind,
And the beat of a clock from a distant floor:
On this scene enter – winged, horned, and spined –
A longlegs, a moth, and a dumbledore;
While 'mid my page there idly stands
A sleepy fly, that rubs its hands . . .

II

Thus meet we five, in this still place,
At this point of time, at this point in space.
– My guests besmear my new-penned line,
Or bang at the lamp and fall supine.
'God's humblest, they!' I muse. Yet why?
They know Earth-secrets that know not I.

Max Gate, 1899

The Darkling Thrush

I leant upon a coppice gate
    When Frost was spectre-gray,
And Winter's dregs made desolate
    The weakening eye of day.
The tangled bine-stems scored the sky
    Like strings of broken lyres,
And all mankind that haunted nigh
    Had sought their household fires.

The land's sharp features seemed to be
    The Century's corpse outleant,
His crypt the cloudy canopy,
    The wind his death-lament.
The ancient pulse of germ and birth
    Was shrunken hard and dry,
And every spirit upon earth
    Seemed fervourless as I.

At once a voice arose among
    The bleak twigs overhead
In a full-hearted evensong
    Of joy illimited;
An aged thrush, frail, gaunt, and small,
    In blast-beruffled plume,
Had chosen thus to fling his soul
    Upon the growing gloom.

16

So little cause for carolings
    Of such ecstatic sound
Was written on terrestrial things
    Afar or nigh around,
That I could think there trembled through
    His happy good-night air
Some blessed Hope, whereof he knew
    And I was unaware.

31 December 1900

The Comet at Yell'ham

I

It bends far over Yell'ham Plain,
   And we, from Yell'ham Height,
Stand and regard its fiery train,
   So soon to swim from sight.

II

It will return long years hence, when
   As now its strange swift shine
Will fall on Yell'ham; but not then
   On that sweet form of thine.

The Ruined Maid

'O 'Melia, my dear, this does everything crown!
Who could have supposed I should meet you in Town?
And whence such fair garments, such prosperi-ty?' –
'O didn't you know I'd been ruined?' said she.

– 'You left us in tatters, without shoes or socks,
Tired of digging potatoes, and spudding up docks;
And now you've gay bracelets and bright feathers three.' –
'Yes: that's how we dress when we're ruined,' said she.

– 'At home in the barton you said "thee" and "thou",
And "thik oon", and "theäs oon", and "t'other"; but now
Your talking quite fits 'ee for high compa-ny!' –
'Some polish is gained with one's ruin,' said she.

– 'Your hands were like paws then, your face blue and bleak,
But now I'm bewitched by your delicate cheek,
And your little gloves fit as on any la-dy!' –
'We never do work when we're ruined,' said she.

– 'You used to call home-life a hag-ridden dream,
And you'd sigh, and you'd sock; but at present you seem
To know not of megrims or melancho-ly!' –
'True. One's pretty lively when ruined,' said she.

– 'I wish I had feathers, a fine sweeping gown,
And a delicate face, and could strut about Town!' –
'My dear – a raw country girl, such as you be,
Cannot quite expect that. You ain't ruined,' said she.

Westbourne Park Villas, 1866

The Self-Unseeing

Here is the ancient floor,
Footworn and hollowed and thin,
Here was the former door
Where the dead feet walked in.

She sat here in her chair,
Smiling into the fire;
He who played stood there,
Bowing it higher and higher.

Childlike, I danced in a dream;
Blessings emblazoned that day;
Everything glowed with a gleam;
Yet we were looking away!

Tess's Lament

I

I would that folk forgot me quite,
    Forgot me quite!
I would that I could shrink from sight,
   And no more see the sun.
Would it were time to say farewell,
To claim my nook, to need my knell,
Time for them all to stand and tell
   O' my day's work as done.

II

Ah! dairy where I lived so long,
    I lived so long;
Where I would rise up stanch and strong,
And lie down hopefully.
'Twas there within the chimney-seat
He watched me to the clock's slow beat —
Loved me, and learnt to call me Sweet,
   And whispered words to me.

III

And now he's gone; and now he's gone; . . .
    And now he's gone!
The flowers we potted p'rhaps are thrown
   To rot upon the farm.
And where we had our supper-fire
May now grow nettle, dock, and briar,
And all the place be mould and mire
   So cozy once and warm.

IV

And it was I who did it all,
        Who did it all;
'Twas I who made the blow to fall
    On him who thought no guile.
Well, it is finished – past, and he
Has left me to my misery,
And I must take my Cross on me,
    For wronging him awhile.

V

How gay we looked that day we wed,
        That day we wed!
'My joy be with ye!' all o'us said
    Astanding by the durn.
I wonder what they say o's now,
And if they know my lot; and how
She feels who milks my favourite cow,
    And takes my place at churn!

VI

It wears me out to think of it,
        To think of it;
I cannot bear my fate as writ,
    I'd have my life unbe;
Would turn my memory to a blot,
Make every relic of me rot,
My doings be as they were not,
    And gone all trace of me!

A Trampwoman's Tragedy
(182–)

I

From Wynyard's Gap the livelong day,
    The livelong day,
We beat afoot the northward way
    We had travelled times before.
The sun-blaze burning on our backs,
Our shoulders sticking to our packs,
By fosseway, fields, and turnpike tracks
    We skirted sad Sedge-Moor.

II

Full twenty miles we jaunted on,
    We jaunted on, –
My fancy-man, and jeering John,
    And Mother Lee, and I.
And, as the sun drew down to west,
We climbed the toilsome Poldon crest,
And saw, of landskip sights the best,
    The inn that beamed thereby.

III

For months we had padded side by side,
    Ay, side by side
Through the Great Forest, Blackmoor wide,
    And where the Parret ran.
We'd faced the gusts on Mendip ridge,
Had crossed the Yeo unhelped by bridge,
Been stung by every Marshwood midge,
    I and my fancy-man.

Lone inns we loved, my man and I,
    My man and I;
'King's Stag', 'Windwhistle' high and dry,
   'The Horse' on Hintock Green,
The cosy house at Wynyard's Gap,
'The Hut' renowned on Bredy Knap,
And many another wayside tap
   Where folk might sit unseen.

V

Now as we trudged – O deadly day,
    O deadly day! –
I teased my fancy-man in play
   And wanton idleness.
I walked alongside jeering John,
I laid his hand my waist upon;
I would not bend my glances on
   My lover's dark distress.

VI

Thus Poldon top at last we won,
    At last we won,
And gained the inn at sink of sun
   Far-famed as 'Marshal's Elm'.
Beneath us figured tor and lea,
From Mendip to the western sea –
I doubt if finer sight there be
   Within this royal realm.

VII

Inside the settle all a-row –
    All four a-row
We sat, I next to John, to show

That he had wooed and won.
And then he took me on his knee,
And swore it was his turn to be
My favoured mate, and Mother Lee
    Passed to my former one.

VIII

Then in a voice I had never heard,
        I had never heard,
My only Love to me: 'One word,
    My lady, if you please!
Whose is the child you are like to bear? –
His? After all my months o' care?'
God knows 'twas not! But, O despair!
    I nodded – still to tease.

IX

Then up he sprung, and with his knife –
        And with his knife
He let out jeering Johnny's life,
    Yes; there, at set of sun.
The slant ray through the window nigh
Gilded John's blood and glazing eye,
Ere scarcely Mother Lee and I
    Knew that the deed was done.

X

The taverns tell the gloomy tale,
        The gloomy tale,
How that at Ivel-chester jail
    My Love, my sweetheart swung;
Though stained till now by no misdeed
Save one horse ta'en in time o' need;
(Blue Jimmy stole right many a steed
    Ere his last fling he flung).

XI

Thereaft I walked the world alone,
　　Alone, alone!
On his death-day I gave my groan
　　And dropt his dead-born child.
'Twas nigh the jail, beneath a tree,
None tending me; for Mother Lee
Had died at Glaston, leaving me
　　Unfriended on the wild.

XII

And in the night as I lay weak,
　　As I lay weak,
The leaves a-falling on my cheek,
　　The red moon low declined –
The ghost of him I'd die to kiss
Rose up and said: 'Ah, tell me this!
Was the child mine, or was it his?
　　Speak, that I rest may find!'

XIII

O doubt not but I told him then,
　　I told him then,
That I had kept me from all men
　　Since we joined lips and swore.
Whereat he smiled, and thinned away
As the wind stirred to call up day . . .
– 'Tis past! And here alone I stray
　　Haunting the Western Moor.

April 1902

A Sunday Morning Tragedy

(*circa* 186–)

I bore a daughter flower-fair,
In Pydel Vale, alas for me;
I joyed to mother one so rare,
But dead and gone I now would be.

Men looked and loved her as she grew,
And she was won, alas for me;
She told me nothing, but I knew,
And saw that sorrow was to be.

I knew that one had made her thrall,
A thrall to him, alas for me;
And then, at last, she told me all,
And wondered what her end would be.

She owned that she had loved too well,
Had loved too well, unhappy she,
And bore a secret time would tell,
Though in her shroud she'd sooner be.

I plodded to her sweetheart's door
In Pydel Vale, alas for me:
I pleaded with him, pleaded sore,
To save her from her misery.

He frowned, and swore he could not wed,
Seven times he swore it could not be;
'Poverty's worse than shame,' he said,
Till all my hope went out of me.

'I've packed my traps to sail the main' –
Roughly he spake, alas did he –
'Wessex beholds me not again,
'Tis worse than any jail would be!'

– There was a shepherd whom I knew,
A subtle man, alas for me:
I sought him all the pastures through,
Though better I had ceased to be.

I traced him by his lantern light,
And gave him hint, alas for me,
Of how she found her in the plight
That is so scorned in Christendie.

'Is there an herb . . . ?' I asked. 'Or none?'
Yes, thus I asked him desperately.
' – There is,' he said; 'a certain one . . .'
Would he had sworn that none knew he!

'To-morrow I will walk your way,'
He hinted low, alas for me. –
Fieldwards I gazed throughout next day;
Now fields I never more would see!

The sunset-shine, as curfew strook,
As curfew strook beyond the lea,
Lit his white smock and gleaming crook,
While slowly he drew near to me.

He pulled from underneath his smock
The herb I sought, my curse to be –
'At times I use it in my flock,'
He said, and hope waxed strong in me.

' 'Tis meant to balk ill-motherings' –
(Ill-motherings! Why should they be?) –
'If not, would God have sent such things?'
So spoke the shepherd unto me.

That night I watched the poppling brew,
With bended back and hand on knee:
I stirred it till the dawnlight grew,
And the wind whiffled wailfully.

'This scandal shall be slain,' said I,
'That lours upon her innocency:
I'll give all whispering tongues the lie;' –
But worse than whispers was to be.

'Here's physic for untimely fruit,'
I said to her, alas for me,
Early that morn in fond salute;
And in my grave I now would be.

– Nest Sunday came, with sweet church chimes
In Pydel Vale, alas for me:
I went into her room betimes;
No more may such a Sunday be!

'Mother, instead of rescue nigh,'
She faintly breathed, alas for me,
'I feel as I were like to die,
And underground soon, soon should be.'

From church that noon the people walked
In twos and threes, alas for me,
Showed their new raiment – smiled and talked,
Though sackcloth-clad I longed to be.

Came to my door her lover's friends,
And cheerly cried, alas for me,
'Right glad are we he makes amends,
For never a sweeter bride can be.'

My mouth dried, as 'twere scorched within,
Dried at their words, alas for me:
More and more neighbours crowded in,
(O why should mothers ever be!)

'Ha-ha! Such well-kept news!' laughed they,
Yes – so they laughed, alas for me.
'Whose banns were called in church today?' –
Christ, how I wished my soul could flee!

'Where is she? O the stealthy miss,'
Still bantered they, alas for me,
'To keep a wedding close as this. . . .'
Ay, Fortune worked thus wantonly!

'But you are pale – you did not know?'
They archly asked, alas for me,
I stammered, 'Yes – some days – ago,'
While coffined clay I wished to be.

' 'Twas done to please her, we surmise?'
(They spoke quite lightly in their glee)
'Done by him as a fond surprise?'
I thought their words would madden me.

Her lover entered. 'Where's my bird? –
My bird – my flower – my picotee?
First time of asking, soon the third!'
Ah, in my grave I well may be.

To me he whispered: 'Since your call –'
So spoke he then, alas for me –
'I've felt for her, and righted all.'
– I think of it to agony.

'She's faint to-day – tired – nothing more –'
Thus did I lie, alas for me. . . .
I called her at her chamber door
As one who scarce had strength to be.

No voice replied. I went within –
O woman! scourged the worst are we. . . .
I shrieked. The others hastened in
And saw the stroke there dealt on me.

There she lay – silent, breathless, dead,
Stone-dead she lay – wronged, sinless she! –
Ghost-white the cheeks once rosy-red:
Death had took her. Death took not me.

I kissed her colding face and hair,
I kissed her corpse – the bride to be! –
My punishment I cannot bear,
But pray God *not* to pity me.

January 1904

Shut Out That Moon

Close up the casement, draw the blind,
　Shut out that stealing moon,
She wears too much the guise she wore
　Before our lutes were strewn
With years-deep dust, and names we read
　On a white stone were hewn.

Step not forth on the dew-dashed lawn
　To view the Lady's Chair,
Immense Orion's glittering form,
　The Less and Greater Bear:
Stay in; to such sights we were drawn
　When faded ones were fair.

Brush not the bough for midnight scents
　That come forth lingeringly,
And wake the same sweet sentiments
　They breathed to you and me
When living seemed a laugh, and love
　All it was said to be.

Within the common lamp-lit room
　Prison my eyes and thought;
Let dingy details crudely loom,
　Mechanic speech be wrought:
Too fragrant was Life's early bloom,
　Too tart the fruit it brought!

1904

The Conformers

Yes; we'll wed, my little fay,
   And you shall write you mine,
And in a villa chastely gray
   We'll house, and sleep, and dine.
   But those night-screened, divine,
   Stolen trysts of heretofore,
We of choice ecstasies and fine
      Shall know no more.

The formal faced cohue
   Will then no more upbraid
With smiting smiles and whisperings two
   Who have thrown less loves in shade.
   We shall no more evade
   The searching light of the sun,
Our game of passion will be played,
      Our dreaming done.

We shall not go in stealth
   To rendezvous unknown,
But friends will ask me of your health,
   And you about my own.
   When we abide alone,
   No leapings each to each,
But syllables in frigid tone
      Of household speech.

When down to dust we glide
   Men will not say askance,
As now: 'How all the country side
   Rings with their mad romance!'
   But as they graveward glance
   Remark: 'In them we lose
A worthy pair, who helped advance
      Sound parish views.'

He Abjures Love

At last I put off love,
    For twice ten years
The daysman of my thought,
    And hope, and doing;
Being ashamed thereof,
    And faint of fears
And desolations, wrought
    In his pursuing,

Since first in youthtime those
    Disquietings
That heart-enslavement brings
    To hale and hoary,
Become my housefellows,
    And, fool and blind,
I turned from kith and kind
    To give him glory.

I was as children be
    Who have no care;
I did not shrink or sigh,
    I did not sicken;
But lo, Love beckoned me,
    And I was bare,
And poor, and starved, and dry,
    And fever-stricken.

Too many times ablaze
    With fatuous fires,
Enkindled by his wiles
    To new embraces,
Did I, by wilful ways
    And baseless ires,
Return the anxious smiles
    Of friendly faces.

No more will now rate I
   The common rare,
The midnight drizzle dew,
   The gray hour golden,
The wind a yearning cry,
   The faulty fair,
Things dreamt, of comelier hue
   Than things beholden! . . .

– I speak as one who plumbs
   Life's dim profound,
One who at length can sound
   Clear views and certain.
But – after love what comes?
   A scene that lours,
A few sad vacant hours,
   And then, the Curtain.

1883

The Pine Planters

(*Marty South's Reverie*)

I

We work here together
  In blast and breeze;
He fills the earth in,
  I hold the trees.

He does not notice
  That what I do
Keeps me from moving
  And chills me through.

He has seen one fairer
  I feel by his eye,
Which skims me as though
  I were not by.

And since she passed here
  He scarce has known
But that the woodland
  Holds him alone.

I have worked here with him
  Since morning shine,
He busy with his thoughts
  And I with mine.

I have helped him so many,
  So many days,
But never win any
  Small word of praise!

Shall I not sigh to him
  That I work on
Glad to be nigh to him
  Though hope is gone?

Nay, though he never
   Knew love like mine,
I'll bear it ever
   And make no sign!

II

From the bundle at hand here
   I take each tree,
And set it to stand, here
   Always to be;
When, in a second,
   As if from fear
Of Life unreckoned
   Beginning here,
It starts a sighing
   Through day and night,
Though while there lying
   'Twas voiceless quite.

It will sigh in the morning,
   Will sigh at noon,
At the winter's warning,
   In wafts of June;
Grieving that never
   Kind Fate decreed
It should for ever
   Remain a seed,
And shun the welter
   Of things without,
Unneeding shelter
   From storm and drought.

Thus, all unknowing
   For whom or what
We set it growing
   In this bleak spot,

It still will grieve here
    Throughout its time,
Unable to leave here,
    Or change its clime;
Or tell the story
    Of us to-day
When, halt and hoary,
    We pass away.

In Front of the Landscape

Plunging and labouring on in a tide of visions,
    Dolorous and dear,
Forward I pushed my way as amid waste waters
    Stretching around,
Through whose eddies there glimmered the customed
  landscape
    Yonder and near

Blotted to feeble mist. And the coomb and the upland
    Coppice-crowned,
Ancient chalk-pit, milestone, rills in the grass-flat
    Stroked by the light,
Seemed but a ghost-like gauze, and no substantial
    Meadow or mound.

What were the infinite spectacles featuring foremost
    Under my sight,
Hindering me to discern my paced advancement
    Lengthening to miles;
What were the re-creations killing the daytime
    As by the night?

O they were speechful faces, gazing insistent,
    Some as with smiles,
Some as with slow-born tears that brinily trundled
    Over the wrecked
Cheeks that were fair in their flush-time, ash now with
  anguish,
    Harrowed by wiles.

Yes, I could see them, feel them, hear them, address them –
    Halo-bedecked –
And, alas, onwards, shaken by fierce unreason,
    Rigid in hate,
Smitten by years-long wryness born of misprision,
    Dreaded, suspect.

Then there would breast me shining sights, sweet seasons
    Further in date;
Instruments of strings with the tenderest passion
    Vibrant, beside
Lamps long extinguished, robes, cheeks, eyes with the earth's
crust
    Now corporate.

Also there rose a headland of hoary aspect
    Gnawed by the tide,
Frilled by the nimb of the morning as two friends stood there
    Guilelessly glad –
Wherefore they knew not – touched by the fringe of an
ecstasy
    Scantly descried.

Later images too did the day unfurl me,
    Shadowed and sad,
Clay cadavers of those who had shared in the dramas,
    Laid now at ease,
Passions all spent, chiefest the one of the broad brow
    Sepulture-clad.

So did beset me scenes miscalled of the bygone,
    Over the leaze,
Past the clump, and down to where lay the beheld ones;
    – Yea, as the rhyme
Sung by the sea-swell, so in their pleading dumbness
    Captured me these.

For, their lost revisiting manifestations
    In their live time
Much had I slighted, caring not for their purport,
    Seeing behind
Things more coveted, reckoned the better worth calling
    Sweet, sad, sublime.

Thus do they now show hourly before the intenser
    Stare of the mind
As they were ghosts avenging their slights by my bypast
    Body-borne eyes,
Show, too, with fuller translation than rested upon them
    As living kind.

Hence wag the tongues of the passing people, saying
    In their surmise,
'Ah – whose is this dull form that perambulates, seeing
  nought
    Round him that looms
Whithersoever his footsteps turn in his farings,
    Save a few tombs?'

Channel Firing

That night your great guns, unawares,
Shook all our coffins as we lay,
And broke the chancel window-squares,
We thought it was the Judgment-day

And sat upright. While drearisome
Arose the howl of wakened hounds:
The mouse let fall the altar-crumb,
The worms drew back into the mounds,

The glebe cow drooled. Till God called, 'No;
It's gunnery practice out at sea
Just as before you went below;
The world is as it used to be:

'All nations striving strong to make
Red war yet redder. Mad as hatters
They do no more for Christés sake
Than you who are helpless in such matters.

'That this is not the judgment-hour
For some of them's a blessed thing,
For if it were they'd have to scour
Hell's floor for so much threatening. . . .

'Ha, ha. It will be warmer when
I blow the trumpet (if indeed
I ever do; for you are men,
And rest eternal sorely need).'

So down we lay again. 'I wonder,
Will the world ever saner be,'
Said one, 'than when He sent us under
In our indifferent century!'

And many a skeleton shook his head.
'Instead of preaching forty year,'
My neighbour Parson Thirdly said,
'I wish I had stuck to pipes and beer.'

Again the guns disturbed the hour,
Roaring their readiness to avenge,
As far inland as Stourton Tower,
And Camelot, and starlit Stonehenge.

April 1914

The Convergence of the Twain

(*Lines on the loss of the 'Titanic'*)

I

In a solitude of the sea
Deep from human vanity,
And the Pride of Life that planned her, stilly couches she.

II

Steel chambers, late the pyres
Of her salamandrine fires,
Cold currents thrid, and turn to rhythmic tidal lyres.

III

Over the mirrors meant
To glass the opulent
The sea-worm crawls – grotesque, slimed, dumb, indifferent.

IV

Jewels in joy designed
To ravish the sensuous mind
Lie lightless, all their sparkles bleared and black and blind.

V

Dim moon-eyed fishes near
Gaze at the gilded gear
And query: 'What does this vaingloriousness down here?' . . .

VI

Well: while was fashioning
This creature of cleaving wing,
The Immanent Will that stirs and urges everything

VII

      Prepared a sinister mate
      For her – so gaily great –
A Shape of Ice, for the time far and dissociate.

VIII

      And as the smart ship grew
      In stature, grace, and hue,
In shadowy silent distance grew the Iceberg too.

IX

      Alien they seemed to be:
      No mortal eye could see
The intimate welding of their later history,

X

      Or sign that they were bent
      By paths coincident
On being anon twin halves of one august event,

XI

      Till the Spinner of the Years
      Said 'Now!' And each one hears,
And consummation comes, and jars two hemispheres.

1912

Wessex Heights
(1896)

There are some heights in Wessex, shaped as if by a kindly
hand
For thinking, dreaming, dying on, and at crises when I stand,
Say, on Ingpen Beacon eastward, or on Wylls-Neck
westwardly;
I seem where I was before my birth, and after death may be.

In the lowlands I have no comrade, not even the lone man's
friend –
Her who suffereth long and is kind; accepts what he is too
weak to mend:
Down there they are dubious and askance; there nobody
thinks as I,
But mind-chains do not clank where one's next neighbour is
the sky.

In the towns I am tracked by phantoms having weird
detective ways –
Shadows of beings who fellowed with myself of earlier days:
They hang about at places, and they say harsh heavy things –
Men with a wintry sneer, and women with tart disparagings.

Down there I seem to be false to myself, my simple self that
was,
And is not now, and I see him watching, wondering what
crass cause
Can have merged him into such a strange continuator as this,
Who yet has something in common with himself, my
chrysalis.

I cannot go to the great grey Plain; there's a figure against the
moon,
Nobody sees it but I, and it makes my breast beat out of tune;

I cannot go to the tall-spired town, being barred by the forms now passed
For everybody but me, in whose long vision they stand there fast.

There's a ghost at Yell'ham Bottom chiding loud at the fall of the night,
There's ghost in Froom-side Vale, thin-lipped and vague, in a shroud of white,
There is one in the railway train whenever I do not want it near,
I see its profile against the pane, saying what I would not hear.

As for one rare fair woman, I am now but a thought of hers,
I enter her mind and another thought succeeds me that she prefers;
Yet my love for her in its fulness she herself even did not know;
Well, time cures hearts of tenderness, and now I can let her go.

So I am found on Ingpen Beacon, or on Wylls-Neck to the west,
Or else on homely Bulbarrow, or little Pilsdon Crest,
Where men have never cared to haunt, nor women have walked with me,
And ghosts then keep their distance; and I know some liberty.

In Death Divided

I

I shall rot here, with those whom in their day
  You never knew,
And alien ones who, ere they chilled to clay,
  Met not my view,
Will in your distant grave-place ever neighbour you.

II

No shade of pinnacle or tree or tower,
  While earth endures,
Will fall on my mound and within the hour
  Steal on to yours;
One robin never haunt our two green covertures.

III

Some organ may resound on Sunday noons
  By where you lie,
Some other thrill the panes with other tunes
  Where moulder I;
No selfsame chords compose our common lullaby.

IV

The simply-cut memorial at my head
  Perhaps may take
A rustic form, and that above your bed
  A stately make;
No linking symbol show thereon for our tale's sake.

V

And in the monotonous moils of strained, hard-run
    Humanity,
The eternal tie which binds us twain in one
    No eye will see
Stretching across the miles that sever you from me.

189–

The Going

Why did you give no hint that night
That quickly after the morrow's dawn,
And calmly, as if indifferent quite,
You would close your term here, up and be gone
     Where I could not follow
     With wing of swallow
To gain one glimpse of you ever anon!

     Never to bid good-bye,
     Or lip me the softest call,
Or utter a wish for a word, while I
Saw morning harden upon the wall,
     Unmoved, unknowing
     That your great going
Had place that moment, and altered all.

Why do you make me leave the house
And think for a breath it is you I see
At the end of the alley of bending boughs
Where so often at dusk you used to be;
     Till in darkening dankness
     The yawning blankness
Of the perspective sickens me!

     You were she who abode
     By those red-veined rocks far West,
You were the swan-necked one who rode
Along the beetling Beeny Crest,
     And, reining nigh me,
     Would muse and eye me,
While Life unrolled us its very best.

Why, then, latterly did we not speak,
Did we not think of those days long dead,
And ere your vanishing strive to seek

That time's renewal? We might have said,
    'In this bright spring weather
    We'll visit together
Those places that once we visited.'

    Well, well! All's past amend,
    Unchangeable. It must go.
I seem but a dead man held on end
To sink down soon. . . . O you could not know
    That such swift fleeing
    No soul foreseeing –
Not even I – would undo me so!

December 1912

Your Last Drive

Here by the moorway you returned,
And saw the borough lights ahead
That lit your face – all undiscerned
To be in a week the face of the dead,
And you told of the charm of that haloed view
That never again would beam on you.

And on your left you passed the spot
Where eight days later you were to lie,
And be spoken of as one who was not;
Beholding it with a heedless eye
As alien from you, though under its tree
You soon would halt everlastingly.

I drove not with you. . . . Yet had I sat
At your side that eve I should not have seen
That the countenance I was glancing at
Had a last-time look in the flickering sheen,
Nor have read the writing upon your face,
'I go hence soon to my resting-place;

'You may miss me then. But I shall not know
How many times you visit me there,
Or what your thoughts are, of if you go
There never at all. And I shall not care.
Should you censure me I shall take no heed,
And even your praises no more shall need.'

True: never you'll know. And you will not mind.
But shall I then slight you because of such?
Dear ghost, in the past did you ever find
The thought 'What profit,' move me much?
Yet abides the fact, indeed, the same, –
You are past love, praise, indifference, blame.

December 1912

The Walk

You did not walk with me
Of late to the hill-top tree
   By the gated ways,
   As in earlier days;
   You were weak and lame,
   So you never came,
And I went alone, and I did not mind,
Not thinking of you as left behind.

I walked up there to-day
Just in the former way:
   Surveyed around
   The familiar ground
   By myself again:
   What difference, then?
Only that underlying sense
Of the look of a room on returning thence.

Rain on a Grave

Clouds spout upon her
    Their waters amain
    In ruthless disdain, –
Her who but lately
    Had shivered with pain
As at touch of dishonour
If there had lit on her
So coldly, so straightly
    Such arrows of rain.

One who to shelter
    Her delicate head
Would quicken and quicken
    Each tentative tread
If drops chanced to pelt her
    That summertime spills
    In dust-paven rills
When thunder-clouds thicken
    And birds close their bills.

Would that I lay there
    And she were housed here!
Or better, together
Were folded away there
Exposed to one weather
We both, – who would stray there
When sunny the day there,
    Or evening was clear
    At the prime of the year.

Soon will be growing
    Green blades from her mound,
And daisies be showing
    Like stars on the ground,

Till she form part of them –
Ay – the sweet heart of them,
Loved beyond measure
With a child's pleasure
    All her life's round.

31 January 1913

I Found Her Out There

I found her out there
On a slope few see,
That falls westwardly
To the salt-edged air,
Where the ocean breaks
On the purple strand,
And the hurricane shakes
The solid land.

I brought her here,
And have laid her to rest
In a noiseless nest
No sea beats near.
She will never be stirred
In her loamy cell
By the waves long heard
And loved so well.

So she does not sleep
By those haunted heights
The Atlantic smites
And the blind gales sweep,
Whence she often would gaze
At Dundagel's famed head,
While the dipping blaze
Dyed her face fire-red;

And would sigh at the tale
Of sunk Lyonnesse,
As a wind-tugged tress
Flapped her cheek like a flail;
Or listen at whiles
With a thought-bound brow
To the murmuring miles
She is far from now.

Yet her shade, maybe,
Will creep underground
Till it catch the sound
Of that western sea
As it swells and sobs
Where she once domiciled,
And joy in its throbs
With the heart of a child.

December 1912

Without Ceremony

It was your way, my dear,
To vanish without a word
When callers, friends, or kin
Had left, and I hastened in
To rejoin you, as I inferred.

And when you'd a mind to career
Off anywhere – say to town –
You were all on a sudden gone
Before I had thought thereon,
Or noticed your trunks were down.

So, now that you disappear
For ever in that swift style,
Your meaning seems to me
Just as it used to be:
'Good-bye is not worth while!'

Lament

How she would have loved
A party to-day! –
Bright-hatted and gloved,
With table and tray
And chairs on the lawn
Her smiles would have shone
With welcomings. . . . But
She is shut, she is shut
   From friendship's spell
   In the jailing shell
   Of her tiny cell.

Or she would have reigned
At a dinner to-night
With ardours unfeigned,
And a generous delight;
All in her abode
She'd have freely bestowed
On her guests. . . . But alas,
She is shut under grass
   Where no cups flow,
   Powerless to know
   That it might be so.

And she would have sought
With a child's eager glance
The shy snowdrops brought
By the new year's advance,
And peered in the rime
Of Candlemas-time
For crocuses . . . chanced
It that she were not tranced
   From sights she loved best;
   Wholly possessed
   By an infinite rest!

And we are here staying
Amid these stale things,
Who care not for gaying,
And those junketings
That used so to joy her,
And never to cloy her
As us they cloy! . . . But
She is shut, she is shut
    From the cheer of them, dead
      To all done and said
    In her yew-arched bed.

The Haunter

He does not think that I haunt here nightly:
　　How shall I let him know
That whither his fancy sets him wandering
　　I, too, alertly go? –
Hover and hover a few feet from him
　　Just as I used to do,
But cannot answer the words he lifts me –
　　Only listen thereto!

When I could answer he did not say them:
　　When I could let him know
How I would like to join in his journeys
　　Seldom he wished to go.
Now that he goes and wants me with him
　　More than he used to do,
Never he sees my faithful phantom
　　Though he speaks thereto.

Yes, I companion him to places
　　Only dreamers know,
Where the shy hares print long paces,
　　Where the night rooks go;
Into old aisles where the past is all to him,
　　Close as his shade can do,
Always lacking the power to call to him,
　　Near as I reach thereto!

What a good haunter I am, O tell him!
　　Quickly make him know
If he but sigh since my loss befell him
　　Straight to his side I go.
Tell him a faithful one is doing
　　All that love can do
Still that his path may be worth pursuing,
　　And to bring peace thereto.

The Voice

Woman much missed, how you call to me, call to me,
Saying that now you are not as you were
When you had changed from the one who was all to me,
But as at first, when our day was fair.

Can it be you that I hear? Let me view you, then,
Standing as when I drew near to the town
Where you would wait for me: yes, as I knew you then,
Even to the original air-blue gown!

Or is it only the breeze, in its listlessness
Travelling across the wet mead to me here,
You being ever dissolved to wan wistlessness,
Heard no more again far or near?

   Thus I; faltering forward,
   Leaves around me falling,
Wind oozing thin through the thorn from norward,
   And the woman calling.

December 1912

His Visitor

I come across from Mellstock while the moon wastes weaker
To behold where I lived with you for twenty years and more:
I shall go in the gray, at the passing of the mail-train,
And need no setting open of the long familiar door
     As before.

The change I notice in my once own quarters!
A formal-fashioned border where the daisies used to be,
The rooms new painted, and the pictures altered,
And other cups and saucers, and no cosy nook for tea
     As with me.

I discern the dim faces of the sleep-wrapt servants;
They are not those who tended me through feeble hours and
   strong,
But strangers quite, who never knew my rule here,
Who never saw me painting, never heard my softling song
     Float along.

So I don't want to linger in this re-decked dwelling,
I feel too uneasy at the contrasts I behold,
And I make again for Mellstock to return here never,
And rejoin the roomy silence, and the mute and manifold
     Souls of old.

1913

A Circular

As 'legal representative'
I read a missive not my own,
On new designs the senders give
   For clothes, in tints as shown.

Here figure blouses, gowns for tea,
And presentation-trains of state,
Charming ball-dresses, millinery,
   Warranted up to date.

And this gay-pictured, spring-time shout
Of Fashion, hails what lady proud?
Her who before last year ebbed out
   Was costumed in a shroud.

A Dream or No

Why go to Saint-Juliot? What's Juliot to me?
    Some strange necromancy
    But charmed me to fancy
That much of my life claims the spot as its key.

Yes. I have had dreams of that place in the West,
    And a maiden abiding
    Thereat as in hiding;
Fair-eyed and white-shouldered, broad-browed and
    brown-tressed,

And of how, coastward bound on a night long ago,
    There lonely I found her,
    The sea-birds around her,
And other than nigh things uncaring to know.

So sweet her life there (in my thought has it seemed)
    That quickly she drew me
    To take her unto me,
And lodge her long years with me. Such have I dreamed.

But nought of that maid from Saint-Juliot I see;
    Can she ever have been here,
    And shed her life's sheen here,
The woman I thought a long housemate with me?

Does there even a place like Saint-Juliot exist?
    Or a Vallency Valley
    With stream and leafed alley,
Or Beeny, or Bos with its flounce flinging mist?

    February 1913

65

After a Journey

Hereto I come to view a voiceless ghost;
    Whither, O whither will its whim now draw me?
Up the cliff, down, till I'm lonely, lost,
    And the unseen waters' ejaculations awe me.
Where you will next be there's no knowing,
    Facing round about me everywhere,
        With your nut-coloured hair,
And gray eyes, and rose-flush coming and going.

Yes: I have re-entered your olden haunts at last;
    Through the years, through the dead scenes I have tracked
    you;
What have you now found to say of our past –
    Scanned across the dark space wherein I have lacked you?
Summer gave us sweets, but autumn wrought division?
    Things were not lastly as firstly well
        With us twain, you tell?
But all's closed now, despite Time's derision.

I see what you are doing: you are leading me on
    To the spots we knew when we haunted here together,
The waterfall, above which the mist-bow shone
    At the then fair hour in the then fair weather,
And the cave just under, with a voice still so hollow
    That it seems to call out to me from forty years ago,
        When you were all aglow,
And not the thin ghost that I now frailly follow!

Ignorant of what there is flitting here to see,
    The waked birds preen and the seals flop lazily,
Soon you will have, Dear, to vanish from me,
    For the stars close their shutters and the dawn whitens
        hazily.

Trust me, I mind not, though Life lours,
   The bringing me here; nay, bring me here again!
      I am just the same as when
Our days were a joy, and our paths through flowers.

   Pentargan Bay

A Death-Day Recalled

Beeny did not quiver,
   Juliot grew not gray,
Thin Vallency's river
   Held its wonted way.
Bos seemed not to utter
   Dimmest note of dirge,
Targan mouth a mutter
   To its creamy surge.

Yet though these, unheeding,
   Listless, passed the hour
Of her spirit's speeding,
   She had, in her flower,
Sought and loved the places –
   Much and often pined
For their lonely faces
   When in towns confined.

Why did not Vallency
   In his purl deplore
One whose haunts were whence he
   Drew his limpid store?
Why did Bos not thunder,
   Targan apprehend
Body and Breath were sunder
   Of their former friend?

Beeny Cliff

March 1870–March 1913

I

O the opal and the sapphire of that wandering western sea,
And the woman riding high above with bright hair flapping
    free –
The woman whom I loved so, and who loyally loved me.

II

The pale mews plained below us, and the waves seemed far
    away
In a nether sky, engrossed in saying their ceaseless babbling
    say,
As we laughed light-heartedly aloft on that clear-sunned
    March day.

III

A little cloud then cloaked us, and there flew an irised rain,
And the Atlantic dyed its levels with a dull misfeatured stain,
And then the sun burst out again, and purples prinked the
    main.

IV

– Still in all its chasmal beauty bulks old Beeny to the sky,
And shall she and I not go there once again now March is
    nigh,
And the sweet things said in that March say anew there by
    and by?

V

What if still in chasmal beauty looms that wild weird western
   shore,
The woman now is – elsewhere – whom the ambling pony
   bore,
And nor knows nor cares for Beeny, and will laugh there
   nevermore.

At Castle Boterel

As I drive to the junction of lane and highway,
    And the drizzle bedrenches the waggonette,
I look behind at the fading byway,
    And see on its slope, now glistening wet,
        Distinctly yet

Myself and a girlish form benighted
    In dry March weather. We climb the road
Beside a chaise. We had just alighted
    To ease the sturdy pony's load
        When he sighed and slowed.

What we did as we climbed, and what we talked of
    Matters not much, nor to what it led, –
Something that life will not be balked of
    Without rude reason till hope is dead,
        And feeling fled.

If filled but a minute. But was there ever
    A time of such quality, since or before,
In that hill's story? To one mind never,
    Though it has been climbed, foot-swift, foot-sore,
        By thousands more.

Primaeval rocks form the road's steep border,
    And much have they faced there, first and last,
Of the transitory in Earth's long order;
    But what they record in colour and cast
        Is – that we two passed.

And to me, though Time's unflinching rigour,
    In mindless rote, has ruled from sight
The substance now, one phantom figure
    Remains on the slope, as when that night
        Saw us alight.

I look and see it there, shrinking, shrinking,
   I look back at it amid the rain
For the very last time; for my sand is sinking,
   And I shall traverse old love's domain
     Never again.

March 1913

Places

Nobody says: Ah, that is the place
Where chanced, in the hollow of years ago,
What none of the Three Towns cared to know –
The birth of a little girl of grace –
The sweetest the house saw, first or last;
    Yet it was so
    On that day long past.

Nobody thinks: There, there she lay
In a room by the Hoe, like the bud of a flower,
And listened, just after the bedtime hour,
To the stammering chimes that used to play
The quaint Old Hundred-and-Thirteenth tune
    In Saint Andrew's tower
    Night, morn, and noon.

Nobody calls to mind that here
Upon Boterel Hill, where the waggoners skid,
With cheeks whose airy flush outbid
Fresh fruit in bloom, and free of fear,
She cantered down, as if she must fall
    (Though she never did),
    To the charm of all.

Nay: one there is to whom these things,
That nobody else's mind calls back,
Have a savour that scenes in being lack,
And a presence more than the actual brings;
To whom to-day is beneaped and stale,
    And its urgent clack
    But a vapid tale.

Plymouth, March 1913

The Phantom Horsewoman

I

Queer are the ways of a man I know:
>   He comes and stands
>   In a careworn craze,
>   And looks at the sands
>   And the seaward haze,
>   With moveless hands
>   And face and gaze,
>   Then turns to go . . .
And what does he see when he gazes so?

II

They say he sees as an instant thing
>   More clear than to-day,
>   A sweet soft scene
>   That was once in play
>   By that briny green;
>   Yes, notes alway
>   Warm, real, and keen,
>   What his back years bring –
A phantom of his own figuring.

III

Of this vision of his they might say more:
>   Not only there
>   Does he see this sight,
>   But everywhere
>   In his brain – day, night,
>   As if on the air
>   It were drawn rose bright –
>   Yea, far from that shore
Does he carry this vision of heretofore:

IV

A ghost-girl-rider. And though, toil-tried,
    He withers daily,
    Time touches her not,
    But she still rides gaily
    In his rapt thought
    On that shagged and shaly
    Atlantic spot,
    And as when first eyed
Draws rein and sings to the swing of the tide.

    1913

The Spell of the Rose

'I mean to build a hall anon,
　　And shape two turrets there,
　　And a broad newelled stair,
And a cool well for crystal water;
　　Yes; I will build a hall anon,
　　Plant roses love shall feed upon,
　　And apple trees and pear.'

He set to build the manor-hall,
　　And shaped the turrets there,
　　And the broad newelled stair,
And the cool well for crystal water;
　　He built for me that manor-hall,
　　And planted many trees withal,
　　But no rose anywhere.

And as he planted never a rose
　　That bears the flower of love,
　　Though other flowers throve
Some heart-bane moved our souls to sever
　　Since he had planted never a rose;
　　And misconceits raised horrid shows,
　　And agonies came thereof.

'I'll mend these miseries,' then said I,
　　And so, at dead of night,
　　I went and, screened from sight,
That nought should keep our souls in severance,
　　I set a rose-bush. 'This,' said I,
　　'May end divisions dire and wry,
　　And long-drawn days of blight.'

But I was called from earth – yea, called
　　Before my rose-bush grew;
　　And would that now I knew

What feels he of the tree I planted,
    And whether, after I was called
    To be a ghost, he, as of old,
        Gave me his heart anew!

    Perhaps now blooms that queen of trees
        I set but saw not grow,
        And he, beside its glow –
Eyes couched of the mis-vision that blurred me –
    Ay, there beside that queen of trees
    He sees me as I was, though sees
        Too late to tell me so!

St Launce's Revisited

Slip back, Time!
Yet again I am nearing
Castle and keep, uprearing
Gray, as in my prime.

At the inn
Smiling nigh, why is it
Not as on my visit
When hope and I were twin?

Groom and jade
Whom I found here, moulder;
Strange the tavern-holder,
Strange the tap-maid.

Here I hired
Horse and man for bearing
Me on my wayfaring
To the door desired.

Evening gloomed
As I journeyed forward
To the faces shoreward,
Till their dwelling loomed.

If again
Towards the Atlantic sea there
I should speed, they'd be there
Surely now as then? . . .

Why waste thought,
When I know them vanished
Under earth; yea, banished
Ever into nought!

Where the Picnic Was

Where we made the fire
In the summer time
Of branch and briar
On the hill to the sea,
I slowly climb
Through winter mire,
And scan and trace
The forsaken place
Quite readily.

Now a cold wind blows,
And the grass is gray,
But the spot still shows
As a burnt circle – aye,
And stick-ends, charred,
Still strew the sward
Whereon I stand,
Last relic of the band
Who came that day!

Yes, I am here
Just as last year,
And the sea breathes brine
From its strange straight line
Up hither, the same
As when we four came.
– But two have wandered far
From this grassy rise
Into urban roar
Where no picnics are,
And one – has shut her eyes
For evermore.

In the Servants' Quarters

'Man, you too, aren't you, one of these rough followers of the
      criminal?
All hanging hereabout to gather how he's going to bear
Examination in the hall.' She flung disdainful glances on
The shabby figure standing at the fire with others there,
      Who warmed them by its flare.

'No indeed, my skipping maiden: I know nothing of the trial
      here,
Or criminal, if so he be. – I chanced to come this way,
And the fire shone out into the dawn, and morning airs are
      cold now;
I, too, was drawn in part by charms I see before me play,
      That I see not every day.'

'Ha, ha!' then laughed the constables who also stood to warm
      themselves,
The while another maiden scrutinized his features hard,
As the blaze threw into contrast every line and knot that
      wrinkled them,
Exclaiming, 'Why, last night when he was brought in by the
      guard,
      You were with him in the yard!'

'Nay, nay, you teasing wench, I say! You know you speak
      mistakenly.
Cannot a tired pedestrian who has legged it long and far
Here on his way from northern parts, engrossed in humble
      marketings,
Come in and rest awhile, although judicial doings are
      Afoot by morning star?'

'O, come, come!' laughed the constables. 'Why, man, you
      speak the dialect
He uses in his answers; you can hear him up the stairs.

So own it. We sha'n't hurt ye. There he's speaking now! His
   syllables
Are those you sound yourself when you are talking unawares,
      As this pretty girl declares.'

'And you shudder when his chain clinks!' she rejoined. 'O
   yes, I noticed it.
And you winced, too, when those cuffs they gave him echoed
   to us here.
They'll soon be coming down, and you may then have to
   defend yourself
Unless you hold your tongue, or go away and keep you clear
      When he's led to judgment near!'

'No! I'll be damned in hell if I know anything about the man!
No single thing about him more than everybody knows!
Must not I even warm my hands but I am charged with
   blasphemies?' . . .
– His face convulses as the morning cock that moment
   crows,
      And he droops, and turns, and goes.

Regret Not Me

    Regret not me;
  Beneath the sunny tree
I lie uncaring, slumbering peacefully.

    Swift as the light
  I flew my faery flight;
Ecstatically I moved, and feared no night.

    I did not know
  That heydays fade and go,
But deemed that what was would be always so.

    I skipped at morn
  Between the yellowing corn,
Thinking it good and glorious to be born.

    I ran at eves
  Among the piled-up sheaves,
Dreaming, 'I grieve not, therefore nothing grieves.'

    Now soon will come
  The apple, pear, and plum,
And hinds will sing, and autumn insects hum.

    Again you will fare
  To cider-makings rare,
And junketings; but I shall not be there.

    Yet gaily sing
  Until the pewter ring
Those songs we sang when we went gipsying.

    And lightly dance
  Some triple-timed romance
In coupled figures, and forget mischance;

And mourn not me
Beneath the yellowing tree;
For I shall mind not, slumbering peacefully.

The Abbey Mason

Inventor of the 'Perpendicular' Style of Gothic Architecture
(With Memories of John Hicks, Architect)

The new-vamped Abbey shaped apace
In the fourteenth century of grace;

(The church which, at an after date,
Acquired cathedral rank and state.)

Panel and circumscribing wall
Of latest feature, trim and tall,

Rose roundabout the Norman core
In prouder pose than theretofore,

Encasing magically the old
With parpend ashlars manifold.

The trowels rang out, and tracery
Appeared where blanks had used to be.

Men toiled for pleasure more than pay,
And all went smoothly day by day,

Till, in due course, the transept part
Engrossed the master-mason's art.

– Home-coming thence he tossed and turned
Throughout the night till the new sun burned.

'What fearful visions have inspired
These gaingivings?' his wife inquired;

'As if your tools were in your hand
You have hammered, fitted, muttered, planned;

'You have thumped as you were working hard:
I might have found me bruised and scarred.

84

'What then's amiss? What eating care
Looms nigh, whereof I am unaware?'

He answered not, but churchward went,
Viewing his draughts with discontent;

And fumbled there the livelong day
Till, hollow-eyed, he came away.

– 'Twas said, 'The master-mason's ill!'
And all the abbey works stood still.

Quoth Abbot Wygmore: 'Why, O why
Distress yourself? You'll surely die!'

The mason answered, trouble-torn,
'This long-vogued style is quite outworn!

'The upper archmould nohow serves
To meet the lower tracery curves:

'The ogees bend too far away
To give the flexures interplay.

'This it is causes my distress. . . .
So it will ever be unless

'New forms be found to supersede
The circle when occasions need.

'To carry it out I have tried and toiled,
And now perforce must own me foiled!

'Jeerers will say: "Here was a man
Who could not end what he began!"'

– So passed that day, the next, the next;
The abbot scanned the task, perplexed;

The townsmen mustered all their wit
To fathom how to compass it,

But no raw artistries availed
Where practice in the craft had failed. . . .

– One night he tossed, all open-eyed,
And early left his helpmeet's side.

Scattering the rushes of the floor
He wandered from the chamber door

And sought the sizing pile, whereon
Struck dimly a cadaverous dawn

Through freezing rain, that drenched the board
Of diagram-lines he last had scored –

Chalked phantasies in vain begot
To knife the architectural knot –

In front of which he dully stood,
Regarding them in hopeless mood.

He closelier looked; then looked again:
The chalk-scratched draught-board faced the rain,

Whose icicled drops deformed the lines
Innumerous of his lame designs,

So that they streamed in small white threads
From the upper segments to the heads

Of arcs below, uniting them
Each by a stalactitic stem.

– At once, with eyes that struck out sparks,
He adds accessory cusping-marks,

Then laughs aloud. The thing was done
So long assayed from sun to sun. . . .

– Now in his joy he grew aware
Of one behind him standing there,

And, turning, saw the abbot, who
The weather's whim was watching too.

Onward to Prime the abbot went,
Tacit upon the incident.

– Men now discerned as days revolved
The ogive riddle had been solved;

Templates were cut, fresh lines were chalked
Where lines had been defaced and balked,

And the work swelled and mounted higher,
Achievement distancing desire;

Here jambs with transoms fixed between,
'Where never the like before had been –

There little mullions thinly sawn
Where meeting circles once were drawn.

'We knew,' men said, 'the thing would go
After his craft-wit got aglow,

'And, once fulfilled what he has designed,
We'll honour him and his great mind!'

When matters stood thus poised awhile,
And all surrounding shed a smile,

The master-mason on an eve
Homed to his wife and seemed to grieve. . . .

– 'The abbot spoke to me to-day;
He hangs about the works alway.

'He knows the source as well as I
Of the new style men magnify.

'He said: "You pride yourself too much
On your creation. Is it such?

' "Surely the hand of God it is
That conjured so, and only His! –

' "Disclosing by the frost and rain
Forms your invention chased in vain;

' "Hence the devices deemed so great
You copied, and did not create."

'I feel the abbot's words are just,
And that all thanks renounce I must.

'Can a man welcome praise and pelf
For hatching art that hatched itself? . . .

'So, I shall own the deft design
Is Heaven's outshaping, and not mine.'

'What!' said she. 'Praise your works ensure
To throw away, and quite obscure

'Your beaming and benificent star?
Better you leave things as they are!

'Why, think awhile. Had not your zest
In your loved craft curtailed your rest –

'Had you not gone there ere the day
The sun had melted all away!'

– But, though his good wife argued so,
The mason let the people know

That not unaided sprang the thought
Whereby the glorious fane was wrought,

But that by frost when dawn was dim
The method was disclosed to him.

'Yet,' said the townspeople thereat,
' 'Tis your own doing, even with that!'

But he – chafed, childlike, in extremes –
The temperament of men of dreams –

Aloofly scrupled to admit
That he did aught but borrow it,

And diffidently made request
That with the abbot all should rest.

– As none could doubt the abbot's word,
Or question what the church averred,

The mason was at length believed
Of no more count than he conceived,

And soon began to lose the fame
That late had gathered round his name. . . .

– Time passed, and like a living thing
The pile went on embodying,

And workmen died, and young ones grew,
And the old mason sank from view

And Abbots Wygmore and Staunton went
And Horton sped the embellishment.

But not till years had far progressed
Chanced it that, one day, much impressed,

Standing within the well-graced aisle,
He asked who first conceived the style;

And some decrepit sage detailed
How, when invention nought availed,

The cloud-cast waters in their whim
Came down, and gave the hint to him

Who struck each arc, and made each mould;
And how the abbot would not hold

As sole begetter him who applied
Forms the Almighty sent as guide;

And how the master lost renown,
And wore in death no artist's crown.

– Then Horton, who in inner thought
Had more perceptions than he taught,

Replied: 'Nay; art can but transmute;
Invention is not absolute;

'Things fail to spring from nought at call,
And art-beginnings most of all.

'He did but what all artists do,
Wait upon Nature for his cue.'

– 'Had you been here to tell them so,
Lord Abbot, sixty years ago,

'The mason, now long underground,
Doubtless a different fate had found.

'He passed into oblivion dim,
And none knew what became of him!

'His name? 'Twas of some common kind
And now has faded out of mind.'

The abbot: 'It shall not be hid!
I'll trace it.' . . . But he never did.

– When longer yet dank death had wormed
The brain wherein the style had germed

From Gloucester church it flew afar –
The style called Perpendicular. –

To Winton and to Westminster
It ranged, and grew still beautifuller:

From Solway Frith to Dover Strand
Its fascinations starred the land,

Not only on cathedral walls
But upon courts and castle halls,

Till every edifice in the isle
Was patterned to no other style,

And till, long having played its part
The curtain fell on Gothic art.

– Well: when in Wessex on your rounds,
Take a brief step beyond its bounds,

And enter Gloucester: seek the quoin
Where choir and transept interjoin,

And, gazing at the forms there flung
Against the sky by one unsung –

The ogee arches transom-topped,
The tracery-stalks by spandrels stopped,

Petrified lacework – lightly lined
On ancient massiveness behind –

Muse that some minds so modest be
As to renounce fame's fairest fee,

(Like him who crystallized on this spot
His visionings, but lies forgot,

And many a mediaeval one
Whose symmetries salute the sun)

While others boom a baseless claim,
And upon nothing rear a name.

Exeunt Omnes

I

Everybody else, then, going,
And I still left where the fair was? . . .
Much have I seen of neighbour loungers
   Making a lusty showing,
   Each now past all knowing.

II

There is an air of blankness
In the street and the littered spaces;
Thoroughfare, steeple, bridge and highway
   Wizen themselves to lankness;
   Kennels dribble dankness.

III

Folk all fade. And whither,
As I wait alone where the fair was?
Into the clammy and numbing night-fog
   Whence they entered hither.
   Soon one more goes thither!

2 June 1913

Moments of Vision

That mirror
Which makes of men a transparency,
Who holds that mirror
And bids us such a breast-bare spectacle see
Of you and me?

That mirror
Whose magic penetrates like a dart,
Who lifts that mirror
And throws our mind back on us, and our heart,
Until we start?

That mirror
Works well in these night hours of ache;
Why in that mirror
Are tincts we never see ourselves once take
When the world is awake?

That mirror
Can test each mortal when unaware;
Yea, that strange mirror
May catch his last thoughts, whole life foul or fair,
Glassing it – where?

At the Word 'Farewell'

She looked like a bird from a cloud
   On the clammy lawn,
Moving alone, bare-browed
   In the dim of dawn.
The candles alight in the room
   For my parting meal
Made all things withoutdoors loom
   Strange, ghostly, unreal.

The hour itself was a ghost,
   And it seemed to me then
As of chances the chance furthermost
   I should see her again.
I beheld not where all was so fleet
   That a Plan of the past
Which had ruled us from birthtime to meet
   Was in working at last:

No prelude did I there perceive
   To a drama at all,
Or foreshadow what fortune might weave
   From beginnings so small;
But I rose as if quicked by a spur
   I was bound to obey,
And stepped through the casement to her
   Still alone in the gray.

'I am leaving you. . . . Farewell!' I said,
   As I followed her on
By an alley bare boughs overspread;
   'I soon must be gone!'
Even then the scale might have been turned
   Against love by a feather,
– But crimson one cheek of hers burned
   When we came in together.

First Sight of Her and After

A day is drawing to its fall
   I had not dreamed to see;
The first of many to enthrall
   My spirit, will it be?
Or is this eve the end of all
   Such new delight for me?

I journey home: the pattern grows
   Of moonshades on the way:
'Soon the first quarter, I suppose,'
   Sky-glancing travellers say;
I realize that it, for those,
   Has been a common day.

Heredity

I am the family face;
Flesh perishes, I live on,
Projecting trait and trace
Through time to times anon,
And leaping from place to place
Over oblivion.

The years-heired feature that can
In curve and voice and eye
Despise the human span
Of durance – that is I;
The eternal thing in man,
That heeds no call to die.

Quid Hic Agis?

I

When I weekly knew
An ancient pew,
And murmured there
The forms of prayer
And thanks and praise
In the ancient ways,
And heard read out
During August drought
That chapter from Kings
Harvest-time brings;
– How the prophet, broken
By griefs unspoken,
Went heavily away
To fast and to pray,
And, while waiting to die,
The Lord passed by,
And a whirlwind and fire
Drew nigher and nigher,
And a small voice anon
Bade him up and be gone, –
I did not apprehend
As I sat to the end
And watched for her smile
Across the sunned aisle,
That this tale of a seer
Which came once a year
Might, when sands were heaping,
Be like a sweat creeping,
Or in any degree
Bear on her or on me!

When later, by chance
Of circumstance,
It befel me to read
On a hot afternoon
At the lectern there
The selfsame words
As the lesson decreed,
To the gathered few
From the hamlets near –
Folk of flocks and herds
Sitting half aswoon,
Who listened thereto
As women and men
Not overmuch
Concerned at such –
So, like them then,
I did not see
What drought might be
With me, with her,
As the Kalendar
Moved on, and Time
Devoured our prime.

III

But now, at last,
When our glory has passed,
And there is no smile
From her in the aisle,
But where it once shone
A marble, men say,
With her name thereon
Is discerned to-day;
And spiritless
In the wilderness

I shrink from sight
And desire the night,
(Though, as in old wise,
I might still arise,
Go forth, and stand
And prophesy in the land),
I feel the shake
Of wind and earthquake,
And consuming fire
Nigher and nigher,
And the voice catch clear,
'What doest thou here?'

The Spectator: 1916. During the War

On a Midsummer Eve

I idly cut a parsley stalk,
And blew therein towards the moon;
I had not thought what ghosts would walk
With shivering footsteps to my tune.

I went, and knelt, and scooped my hand
As if to drink, into the brook,
And a faint figure seemed to stand
Above me, with the bygone look.

I lipped rough rhymes of chance, not choice,
I thought not what my words might be;
There came into my ear a voice
That turned a tenderer verse for me.

To My Father's Violin

Does he want you down there
In the Nether Glooms where
The hours may be a dragging load upon him,
    As he hears the axle grind
        Round and round
    Of the great world, in the blind
        Still profound
Of the night-time? He might liven at the sound
Of your string, revealing you had not forgone him.

In the gallery west the nave,
    But a few yards from his grave,
Did you, tucked beneath his chin, to his bowing
    Guide the homely harmony
        Of the quire
    Who for long years strenuously –
        Son and sire –
Caught the strains that at his fingering low or higher
From your four thin threads and eff-holes came outflowing.

And, too, what merry tunes
    He would bow at nights or noons
That chanced to find him bent to lute a measure,
    When he made you speak his heart
        As in dream,
    Without book or music-chart,
        On some theme
Elusive as a jack-o'-lanthorn's gleam,
And the psalm of duty shelved for trill of pleasure.

Well, you can not, alas,
    The barrier overpass
That screens him in those Mournful Meads hereunder,
    Where no fiddling can be heard

In the glades
Of silentness, no bird
Thrills the shades;
Where no viol is touched for songs or serenades,
No bowing wakes a congregation's wonder.

He must do without you now,
Stir you no more anyhow
To yearning concords taught you in your glory;
While, your strings a tangled wreck,
Once smart drawn,
Ten worm-wounds in your neck,
Purflings wan
With dust-hoar, here alone I sadly con
Your present dumbness, shape your olden story.

1916

The Change

Out of the past there rises a week –
  Who shall read the years O! –
Out of the past there rises a week
  Enringed with a purple zone.
Out of the past there rises a week
  When thoughts were strung too thick to speak,
And the magic of its lineaments remains with me alone.

In that week there was heard a singing –
  Who shall spell the years, the years! –
In that week there was heard a singing,
  And the white owl wondered why.
In that week, yea, a voice was ringing,
  And forth from the casement were candles flinging
Radiance that fell on the deodar and lit up the path thereby.

Could that song have a mocking note? –
  Who shall unroll the years O! –
Could that song have a mocking note
  To the white owl's sense as it fell?
Could that song have a mocking note
  As it trilled out warm from the singer's throat,
And who was the mocker and who the mocked when two felt
    all was well?

In a tedious trampling crowd yet later –
  Who shall bare the years, the years! –
In a tedious trampling crowd yet later,
  When silvery singings were dumb;
In a crowd uncaring what time might fate her,
  Mid murks of night I stood to await her,
And the twanging of iron wheels gave out the signal that she
    was come.

She said with a travel-tired smile –
    Who shall lift the years O! –
She said with a travel-tired smile,
    Half scared by scene so strange;
She said, outworn by mile on mile,
The blurred lamps wanning her face the while,
'O Love, I am here; I am with you!' . . . Ah, that there should
      have come a change!

O the doom by someone spoken –
    Who shall unseal the years, the years! –
O the doom that gave no token,
    When nothing of bale saw we:
O the doom by someone spoken,
O the heart by someone broken,
The heart whose sweet reverberances are all time leaves to me.

January–February 1913

In the Seventies

'Qui deridetur ab amico suo sicut ego.' – JOB

In the seventies I was bearing in my breast,
    Penned tight,
Certain starry thoughts that threw a magic light
On the worktimes and the soundless hours of rest
In the seventies; aye, I bore them in my breast
    Penned tight.

In the seventies when my neighbours – even my friend –
    Saw me pass,
Heads were shaken, and I heard the words, 'Alas,
For his onward years and name unless he mend!'
In the seventies, when my neighbours and my friend
    Saw me pass.

In the seventies those who met me did not know
    Of the vision
That immuned me from the chillings of misprision
And the damps that choked my goings to and fro
In the seventies; yea, those nodders did not know
    Of the vision.

In the seventies nought could darken or destroy it,
    Locked in me,
Though as delicate as lamp-worm's lucency;
Neither mist nor murk could weaken or alloy it
In the seventies! – could not darken or destroy it,
    Locked in me.

The Oxen

Christmas Eve, and twelve of the clock.
　'Now they are all on their knees,'
An elder said as we sat in a flock
　By the embers in hearthside ease.

We pictured the meek mild creatures where
　They dwelt in their strawy pen,
Nor did it occur to one of us there
　To doubt they were kneeling then.

So fair a fancy few would weave
　In these years! Yet, I feel,
If someone said on Christmas Eve,
　'Come; see the oxen kneel

'In the lonely barton by yonder coomb
　Our childhood used to know,'
I should go with him in the gloom,
　Hoping it might be so.

　1915

Transformations

Portion of this yew
Is a man my grandsire knew,
Bosomed here at its foot:
This branch may be his wife,
A ruddy human life
Now turned to a green shoot.

These grasses must be made
Of her who often prayed,
Last century, for repose;
And the fair girl long ago
Whom I often tried to know
May be entering this rose.

So, they are not underground,
But as nerves and veins abound
In the growths of upper air,
And they feel the sun and rain,
And the energy again
That made them what they were!

The Last Signal

(11 Oct. 1886)

A Memory of William Barnes

Silently I footed by an uphill road
  That led from my abode to a spot yew-boughed;
Yellowly the sun sloped low down to westward,
    And dark was the east with cloud.

Then, amid the shadow of that livid sad east,
  Where the light was least, and a gate stood wide,
Something flashed the fire of the sun that was facing it,
    Like a brief blaze on that side.

Looking hard and harder I knew what it meant –
  The sudden shine sent from the livid east scene;
It meant the west mirrored by the coffin of my friend there,
    Turning to the road from his green,

To take his last journey forth – he who in his prime
  Trudged so many a time from that gate athwart the land!
Thus a farewell to me he signalled on his grave-way,
    As with a wave of his hand.

Winterborne-Came Path

Overlooking the River Stour

The swallows flew in the curves of an eight
    Above the river-gleam
    In the wet June's last beam:
Like little crossbows animate
The swallows flew in the curves of an eight
    Above the river-gleam.

Planing up shavings of crystal spray
    A moor-hen darted out
    From the bank thereabout,
And through the stream-shine ripped his way;
Planing up shavings of crystal spray
    A moor-hen darted out.

Closed were the kingcups; and the mead
    Dripped in monotonous green,
    Though the day's morning sheen
Had shown it golden and honeybée'd;
Closed were the kingcups; and the mead
    Dripped in monotonous green.

And never I turned my head, alack,
    While these things met my gaze
    Through the pane's drop-drenched glaze,
To see the more behind my back. . . .
O never I turned, but let, alack,
    These less things hold my gaze!

The Musical Box

Lifelong to be
Seemed the fair colour of the time;
That there was standing shadowed near
A spirit who sang to the gentle chime
Of the self-struck notes, I did not hear,
    I did not see.

Thus did it sing
To the mindless lyre that played indoors
As she came to listen for me without:
'O value what the nonce outpours –
This best of life – that shines about
    Your welcoming!'

I had slowed along
After the torrid hours were done,
Though still the posts and walls and road
Flung back their sense of the hot-faced sun,
And had walked by Stourside Mill, where broad
    Stream-lilies throng.

And I descried
The dusky house that stood apart,
And her, white-muslined, waiting there
In the porch with high-expectant heart,
While still the thin mechanic air
    Went on inside.

At whiles would flit
Swart bats, whose wings, be-webbed and tanned,
Whirred like the wheels of ancient clocks:
She laughed a hailing as she scanned
Me in the gloom, the tuneful box
    Intoning it.

Lifelong to be
I thought it. That there watched hard by
A spirit who sang to the indoor tune,
'O make the most of what is nigh!'
I did not hear in my dull soul-swoon –
    I did not see.

Old Furniture

I know not how it may be with others
    Who sit amid relics of householdry
That date from the days of their mothers' mothers,
    But well I know how it is with me
        Continually.

I see the hands of the generations
    That owned each shiny familiar thing
In play on its knobs and indentations,
    And with its ancient fashioning
        Still dallying:

Hands behind hands, growing paler and paler,
    As in a mirror a candle-flame
Shows images of itself, each frailer
    As it recedes, though the eye may frame
        Its shape the same.

On the clock's dull dial a foggy finger,
    Moving to set the minutes right
With tentative touches that lift and linger
    In the wont of a moth on a summer night,
        Creeps to my sight.

On this old viol, too, fingers are dancing –
    As whilom – just over the strings by the nut,
The tip of a bow receding, advancing
    In airy quivers, as if it would cut
        The plaintive gut.

And I see a face by that box for tinder,
    Glowing forth in fits from the dark,
And fading again, as the linten cinder
    Kindles to red at the flinty spark,
        Or goes out stark.

Well, well. It is best to be up and doing,
  The world has no use for one to-day
Who eyes things thus – no aim pursuing!
  He should not continue in this stay,
    But sink away.

During Wind and Rain

They sing their dearest songs –
He, she, all of them – yea,
Treble and tenor and bass,
    And one to play;
With the candles mooning each face. . . .
      Ah, no; the years O!
How the sick leaves reel down in throngs!

They clear the creeping moss –
Elders and juniors – aye,
Making the pathways neat
    And the garden gay;
And they build a shady seat. . . .
      Ah, no; the years, the years;
See, the white storm-birds wing across!

They are blithely breakfasting all –
Men and maidens – yea,
Under the summer tree,
    With a glimpse of the bay,
While pet fowl come to the knee. . . .
      Ah, no; the years O!
And the rotten rose is ript from the wall.

They change to a high new house,
He, she, all of them – aye,
Clocks and carpets and chairs
    On the lawn all day,
And brightest things that are theirs. . . .
      Ah, no; the years, the years;
Down their carved names the rain-drop ploughs.

Who's in the Next Room?

'Who's in the next room? – who?
    I seemed to see
Somebody in the dawning passing through,
    Unknown to me.'
'Nay: you saw nought. He passed invisibly.'

'Who's in the next room? – who?
    I seem to hear
Somebody muttering firm in a language new
    That chills the ear.'
'No: you catch not his tongue who has entered there.'

'Who's in the next room? – who?
    I seem to feel
His breath like a clammy draught, as if it drew
    From the Polar Wheel.'
'No: none who breathes at all does the door conceal.'

'Who's in the next room? – who?
    A figure wan
With a message to one in there of something due?
    Shall I know him anon?'
'Yea he; and he brought such; and you'll know him anon.'

Midnight on the Great Western

In the third-class seat sat the journeying boy,
   And the roof-lamp's oily flame
Played down on his listless form and face,
Bewrapt past knowing to what he was going,
     Or whence he came.

In the band of his hat the journeying boy
   Had a ticket stuck; and a string
Around his neck bore the key of his box,
That twinkled gleams of the lamp's sad beams
     Like a living thing.

What past can be yours, O journeying boy
   Towards a world unknown,
Who calmly, as if incurious quite
On all at stake, can undertake
     This plunge alone?

Knows your soul a sphere, O journeying boy,
   Our rude realms far above,
Whence with spacious vision you mark and mete
This region of sin that you find you in,
     But are not of?

In a Waiting-Room

On a morning sick as the day of doom
    With the drizzling gray
    Of an English May,
There were few in the railway waiting-room.
About its walls were framed and varnished
Pictures of liners, fly-blown, tarnished.
The table bore a Testament
For travellers' reading, if suchwise bent.

    I read it on and on,
And, thronging the Gospel of Saint John,
Were figures – additions, multiplications –
By some one scrawled, with sundry emendations;
    Not scoffingly designed,
    But with an absent mind, –
Plainly a bagman's counts of cost,
What he had profited, what lost;
And whilst I wondered if there could have been
    Any particle of a soul
    In that poor man at all,
    To cypher rates of wage
    Upon that printed page,
    There joined in the charmless scene
And stood over me and the scribbled book
    (To lend the hour's mean hue
    A smear of tragedy too)
A soldier and wife, with haggard look
Subdued to stone by strong endeavour;
    And then I heard
    From a casual word
They were parting as they believed for ever.

But next there came
Like the eastern flame
Of some high altar, children – a pair –
Who laughed at the fly-blown pictures there.
'Here are the lovely ships that we,
Mother, are by and by going to see!
When we get there it's 'most sure to be fine,
And the band will play, and the sun will shine!'

It rained on the skylight with a din
As we waited and still no train came in;
But the words of the child in the squalid room
Had spread a glory through the gloom.

The Shadow on the Stone

I went by the Druid stone
  That broods in the garden white and lone,
And I stopped and looked at the shifting shadows
  That at some moments fall thereon
  From the tree hard by with a rhythmic swing,
  And they shaped in my imagining
To the shade that a well-known head and shoulders
  Threw there when she was gardening.

I thought her behind my back,
  Yea, her I long had learned to lack,
And I said: 'I am sure you are standing behind me,
  Though how do you get into this old track?'
  And there was no sound but the fall of a leaf
  As a sad response; and to keep down grief
I would not turn my head to discover
  That there was nothing in my belief.

Yet I wanted to look and see
  That nobody stood at the back of me;
But I thought once more: 'Nay, I'll not unvision
  A shape which, somehow, there may be.'
  So I went on softly from the glade,
  And left her behind me throwing her shade,
As she were indeed an apparition –
  My head unturned lest my dream should fade.

Begun 1913: finished 1916

In Time of 'The Breaking of Nations'

I

Only a man harrowing clods
   In a slow silent walk
With an old horse that stumbles and nods
   Half asleep as they stalk.

II

Only thin smoke without flame
   From the heaps of couch-grass;
Yet this will go onward the same
   Though Dynasties pass.

III

Yonder a maid and her wight
   Come whispering by:
War's annals will cloud into night
   Ere their story die.

1915

Afterwards

When the Present has latched its postern behind my
    tremulous stay,
  And the May month flaps its glad green leaves like wings,
Delicate-filmed as new-spun silk, will the neighbours say,
  'He was a man who used to notice such things'?

If it be in the dusk when, like an eyelid's soundless blink,
  The dewfall-hawk comes crossing the shades to alight
Upon the wind-warped upland thorn, a gazer may think,
  'To him this must have been a familiar sight.'

If I pass during some nocturnal blackness, mothy and warm,
  When the hedgehog travels furtively over the lawn,
One may say, 'He strove that such innocent creatures should
    come to no harm,
  But he could do little for them; and now he is gone.'

If, when hearing that I have been stilled at last, they stand at
    the door,
  Watching the full-starred heavens that winter sees,
Will this thought rise on those who will meet my face no
    more,
  'He was one who had an eye for such mysteries'?

And will any say when my bell of quittance is heard in the
    gloom,
  And a crossing breeze cuts a pause in its outrollings,
Till they rise again, as they were a new bell's boom,
  'He hears it not now, but used to notice such things'?

A Jog-Trot Pair

Who were the twain that trod this track
   So many times together
     Hither and back,
In spells of certain and uncertain weather?

Commonplace in conduct they
   Who wandered to and fro here
     Day by day:
Two that few dwellers troubled themselves to know here.

The very gravel-path was prim
   That daily they would follow:
     Borders trim:
Never a wayward sprout, or hump, or hollow.

Trite usages in tamest style
   Had tended to their plighting.
     'It's just worth while,
Perhaps,' they had said. 'And saves much sad good-nighting.'

And petty seemed the happenings
   That ministered to their joyance:
     Simple things,
Onerous to satiate souls, increased their buoyance.

Who could those common people be,
   Of days the plainest, barest?
     They were we;
Yes; happier than the cleverest, smartest, rarest.

A Man Was Drawing Near to Me

On that gray night of mournful drone,
Apart from aught to hear, to see,
I dreamt not that from shires unknown
    In gloom, alone,
    By Halworthy,
A man was drawing near to me.

I'd no concern at anything,
No sense of coming pull-heart play;
Yet, under the silent outspreading
    Of even's wing
    Where Otterham lay,
A man was riding up my way.

I thought of nobody – not of one,
But only of trifles – legends, ghosts –
Though, on the moorland dim and dun
    That travellers shun
    About these coasts,
The man had passed Tresparret Posts.

There was no light at all inland,
Only the seaward pharos-fire,
Nothing to let me understand
    That hard at hand
    By Hennett Byre
The man was getting nigh and nigher.

There was a rumble at the door,
A draught disturbed the drapery,
And but a minute passed before,
    With gaze that bore
    My destiny,
The man revealed himself to me.

The Two Houses

In the heart of night,
  When farers were not near,
The left house said to the house on the right,
'I have marked your rise, O smart newcomer here.'

  Said the right, cold-eyed:
  'Newcomer here I am,
Hence haler than you with cracked old hide,
Loose casements, wormy beams, and doors that jam.

  'Modern my wood,
  My hangings fair of hue;
While my windows open as they should,
And water-pipes thread all my chambers through.

  'Your gear is gray,
  Your face wears furrows untold.'
'– Yours might,' mourned the other, 'if you held, brother,
The Presences from aforetime that I hold.

  'You have not known
  Men's lives, deaths, toils, and teens;
You are but a heap of stick and stone:
A new house has no sense of the have-beens.

  'Void as a drum
  You stand: I am packed with these,
Though, strangely, living dwellers who come
See not the phantoms all my substance sees!

  'Visible in the morning
  Stand they, when dawn drags in;
Visible at night; yet hint or warning
Of these thin elbowers few of the inmates win.

'Babes new-brought-forth
   Obsess my rooms; straight-stretched
Lank corpses, ere outborne to earth;
Yea, throng they as when first from the 'Byss upfetched.

   'Dancers and singers
   Throb in me now as once;
Rich-noted throats and gossamered flingers
Of heels; the learned in love-lore and the dunce.

   'Note here within
   The bridegroom and the bride,
Who smile and greet their friends and kin,
And down my stairs depart for tracks untried.

   'Where such inbe,
   A dwelling's character
Takes theirs, and a vague semblancy
To them in all its limbs, and light, and atmosphere.

   'Yet the blind folk
   My tenants, who come and go
In the flesh mid these, with souls unwoke,
Of such sylph-like surrounders do not know.'

   ' – Will the day come,'
   Said the new one, awestruck, faint,
'When I shall lodge shades dim and dumb –
And with such spectral guests become acquaint?'

   ' – That will it, boy;
   Such shades will people thee,
Each in his misery, irk, or joy,
And print on thee their presences as on me.'

The Fallow Deer at the Lonely House

One without looks in to-night
  Through the curtain-chink
From the sheet of glistening white;
One without looks in to-night
  As we sit and think
  By the fender-brink.

We do not discern those eyes
  Watching in the snow;
Lit by lamps of rosy dyes
We do not discern those eyes
  Wondering, aglow,
  Fourfooted, tiptoe.

At the Railway Station, Upway

'There is not much that I can do,
For I've no money that's quite my own!'
　　Spoke up the pitying child –
A little boy with a violin
At the station before the train came in, –
'But I can play my fiddle to you,
And a nice one 'tis, and good in tone!'

　　The man in the handcuffs smiled;
The constable looked, and he smiled, too,
　　As the fiddle began to twang;
And the man in the handcuffs suddenly sang
　　　　With grimful glee:
　　　　'This life so free
　　　　Is the thing for me!'
And the constable smiled, and said no word,
As if unconscious of what he heard;
And so they went on till the train came in –
The convict, and boy with the violin.

Voices from Things Growing in a Churchyard

These flowers are I, poor Fanny Hurd,
    Sir or Madam,
A little girl here sepultured.
Once I flit-fluttered like a bird
Above the grass, as now I wave
In daisy shapes above my grave,
    All day cheerily,
    All night eerily!

– I am one Bachelor Bowring, 'Gent',
    Sir or Madam;
In shingled oak my bones were pent;
Hence more than a hundred years I spent
In my feat of change from a coffin-thrall
To a dancer in green as leaves on a wall,
    All day cheerily,
    All night eerily!

– I, these berries of juice and gloss,
    Sir or Madam,
Am clean forgotten as Thomas Voss;
Thin-urned, I have burrowed away from the moss
That covers my sod, and have entered this yew,
And turned to clusters ruddy of view,
    All day cheerily,
    All night eerily!

– The Lady Gertrude, proud, high-bred,
    Sir or Madam,
Am I – this laurel that shades your head;
Into its veins I have stilly sped,
And made them of me; and my leaves now shine,
As did my satins superfine,
    All day cheerily,
    All night eerily!

– I, who as innocent withwind climb,
  Sir or Madam,
Am one Eve Greensleeves, in olden time
Kissed by men from many a clime,
Beneath sun, stars, in blaze, in breeze,
As now by glowworms and by bees,
  All day cheerily,
  All night eerily!

– I'm old Squire Audeley Grey, who grew,
  Sir or Madam,
Aweary of life, and in scorn withdrew;
Till anon I clambered up anew
As ivy-green, when my ache was stayed,
And in that attire I have longtime gayed
  All day cheerily,
  All night eerily!

– And so these maskers breathe to each
  Sir or Madam
Who lingers there, and their lively speech
Affords an interpreter much to teach,
As their murmurous accents seem to come
Thence hitheraround in a radiant hum,
  All day cheerily,
  All night eerily!

On the Way

The trees fret fitfully and twist,
Shutters rattle and carpets heave,
Slime is the dust of yestereve,
    And in the streaming mist
Fishes might seem to fin a passage if they list.

        But to his feet,
        Drawing nigh and nigher
        A hidden seat,
        The fog is sweet
        And the wind a lyre.

A vacant sameness grays the sky,
A moisture gathers on each knop
Of the bramble, rounding to a drop,
    That greets the goer-by
With the cold listless lustre of a dead man's eye.

        But to her sight,
        Drawing nigh and nigher
        Its deep delight,
        The fog is bright
        And the wind a lyre.

After a Romantic Day

The railway bore him through
An earthen cutting out from a city:
    There was no scope for view,
Though the frail light shed by a slim young moon
    Fell like a friendly tune.

    Fell like a liquid ditty,
And the blank lack of any charm
    Of landscape did no harm.
The bald steep cutting, rigid, rough,
    And moon-lit, was enough
For poetry of place: its weathered face
Formed a convenient sheet whereon
The visions of his mind were drawn.

A Procession of Dead Days

I see the ghost of a perished day;
I know his face, and the feel of his dawn:
'Twas he who took me far away

　　To a spot strange and gray:
Look at me, Day, and then pass on,
But come again: yes, come anon!

Enters another into view;
His features are not cold or white,
But rosy as a vein seen through:

　　Too soon he smiles adieu.
Adieu, O ghost-day of delight;
But come and grace my dying sight.

Enters the day that brought the kiss:
He brought it in his foggy hand
To where the mumbling river is,

　　And the high clematis;
It lent new colour to the land,
And all the boy within me manned.

Ah, this one. Yes, I know his name,
He is the day that wrought a shine
Even on a precinct common and tame,

　　As 'twere of purposed aim.
He shows him as a rainbow sign
Of promise made to me and mine.

The next stands forth in his morning clothes,
And yet, despite their misty blue,
They mark no sombre custom-growths

　　That joyous living loathes,
But a meteor act, that left in its queue
A train of sparks my lifetime through.

I almost tremble at his nod –
This next in train – who looks at me
As I were slave, and he were god
    Wielding an iron rod.
I close my eyes; yet still is he
In front there, looking mastery.

In semblance of a face averse
The phantom of the next one comes:
I did not know what better or worse
    Chancings might bless or curse
When his original glossed the thrums
Of ivy, bringing that which numbs.

Yes; trees were turning in their sleep
Upon their windy pillows of gray
When he stole in. Silent his creep
    On the grassed eastern steep. . . .
I shall not soon forget that day,
And what his third hour took away!

Without, Not Within Her

It was what you bore with you, Woman,
    Not inly were,
That throned you from all else human,
    However fair!

It was that strange freshness you carried
    Into a soul
Whereon no thought of yours tarried
    Two moments at all.

And out from his spirit flew death,
    And bale, and ban,
Like the corn-chaff under the breath
    Of the winnowing-fan.

The Whitewashed Wall

Why does she turn in that shy soft way
    Whenever she stirs the fire,
And kiss to the chimney-corner wall,
    As if entranced to admire
Its whitewashed bareness more than the sight
    Of a rose in richest green?
I have known her long, but this raptured rite
    I never before have seen.

– Well, once when her son cast his shadow there,
    A friend took a pencil and drew him
Upon that flame-lit wall. And the lines
    Had a lifelike semblance to him.
And there long stayed his familiar look;
    But one day, ere she knew,
The whitener came to cleanse the nook,
    And covered the face from view.

'Yes,' he said: 'My brush goes on with a rush,
    And the draught is buried under;
When you have to whiten old cots and brighten,
    What else can you do, I wonder?'
But she knows he's there. And when she yearns
    For him, deep in the labouring night,
She sees him as close at hand, and turns
    To him under his sheet of white.

Waiting Both

A star looks down at me,
And says: 'Here I and you
Stand, each in his degree:
What do you mean to do, –
    Mean to do?'

I say: 'For all I know,
Wait, and let Time go by,
Till my change come.' – 'Just so,'
The star says: 'So mean I: –
    So mean I.'

Last Look round St Martin's Fair

The sun is like an open furnace door,
Whose round revealed retort confines the roar
    Of fires beyond terrene;
The moon presents the lustre-lacking face
    Of a brass dial gone green,
    Whose hours no eye can trace.
The unsold heathcroppers are driven home
To the shades of the Great Forest whence they come
By men with long cord-waistcoats in brown monochrome.
    The stars break out, and flicker in the breeze,
    It seems, that twitches the trees. –
    From its hot idol soon
The fickle unresting earth has turned to a fresh patroon –
    The cold, now brighter, moon.
    The woman in red, at the nut-stall with the gun,
    Lights up, and still goes on:
    She's redder in the flare-lamp than the sun
    Showed it ere it was gone.
    Her hands are black with loading all the day,
    And yet she treats her labour as 'twere play,
    Tosses her ear-rings, and talks ribaldry
To the young men around as natural gaiety,
    And not a weary work she'd readily stay,
    And never again nut-shooting see,
        Though crying, 'Fire away!'

Why Do I?

Why do I go on doing these things?
    Why not cease?
It is that you are yet in this world of welterings
    And unease,
And that, while so, mechanic repetitions please?

When shall I leave off doing these things? –
    When I hear
You have dropped your dusty cloak and taken you wondrous
        wings
    To another sphere,
Where no pain is: Then shall I hush this dinning gear.

Proud Songsters

The thrushes sing as the sun is going,
And the finches whistle in ones and pairs,
And as it gets dark loud nightingales
    In bushes
Pipe, as they can when April wears,
   As if all Time were theirs.

These are brand-new birds of twelve-months' growing,
Which a year ago, or less than twain,
No finches were, nor nightingales,
    Nor thrushes,
But only particles of grain,
   And earth, and air, and rain.

I Am the One

I am the one whom ringdoves see
    Through chinks in boughs
    When they do not rouse
    In sudden dread,
But stay on cooing, as if they said:
    'Oh; it's only he.'

I am the passer when up-eared hares,
    Stirred as they eat
    The new-sprung wheat,
    Their munch resume
As if they thought: 'He is one for whom
    Nobody cares.'

Wet-eyed mourners glance at me
    As in train they pass
    Along the grass
    To a hollowed spot,
And think: 'No matter; he quizzes not
    Our misery.'

I hear above: 'We stars must lend
    No fierce regard
    To his gaze, so hard
    Bent on us thus, –
Must scathe him not. He is one with us
    Beginning and end.'

Lying Awake

You, Morningtide Star, now are steady-eyed, over the east,
    I know it as if I saw you;
You, Beeches, engrave on the sky your thin twigs, even the
       least;
    Had I paper and pencil I'd draw you.

You, Meadow, are white with your counterpane cover of dew,
    I see it as if I were there;
You, Churchyard, are lightening faint from the shade of the
       yew,
    The names creeping out everywhere.

Childhood among the Ferns

I sat one sprinkling day upon the lea,
Where tall-stemmed ferns spread out luxuriantly,
And nothing but those tall ferns sheltered me.

The rain gained strength, and damped each lopping frond,
Ran down their stalks beside me and beyond,
And shaped slow-creeping rivulets as I conned,

With pride, my spray-roofed house. And though anon
Some drops pierced its green rafters, I sat on,
Making pretence I was not rained upon.

The sun then burst, and brought forth a sweet breath
From the limp ferns as they dried underneath:
I said: 'I could live on here thus till death',

And queried in the green rays as I sate:
'Why should I have to grow to man's estate,
And this afar-noised World perambulate?'

He Resolves to Say No More

O my soul, keep the rest unknown!
It is too like a sound of moan
    When the charnel-eyed
    Pale Horse has nighed:
Yea, none shall gather what I hide!

Why load men's minds with more to bear
That bear already ails to spare?
    From now alway
    Till my last day
What I discern I will not say.

Let Time roll backward if it will;
(Magians who drive the midnight quill
    With brain aglow
    Can see it so,)
What I have learnt no man shall know.

And if my vision range beyond
The blinkered sight of souls in bond,
    – By truth made free –
    I'll let all be,
And show to no man what I see.